Pay to Play

Pay to Play

*How Rod Blagojevich
Turned Political Corruption
into a National Sideshow*

Elizabeth Brackett

IVAN R. DEE
Chicago 2009

www.ivanrdee.com

Photograph of Rod Blagojevich boxing courtesy of Richard Younker; all other photographs by permission of the Associated Press.

Library of Congress Cataloging-in-Publication Data:
Brackett, Elizabeth.
    Pay to play : how Rod Blagojevich turned political corruption into a national sideshow / Elizabeth Brackett.
        p. cm.
    Includes index.
    ISBN 978-1-56663-834-0 (cloth : alk. paper)
    1. Blagojevich, Rod R., 1956– 2. Governors—Illinois—Biography. 3. Illinois—Politics and government—1951– 4. Political corruption—Illinois. I. Title.
F546.4.B55B73 2009
977.3'044092—dc22
[B]   2009010566

For Peter
with love and appreciation
for your patience and support

Contents

Preface

WHEN Rod Blagojevich was catapulted into the national
consciousness it was for far different reasons than he could
ever have imagined. He had long dreamed of achieving
national prominence as President of the United States,
not as a man who had become a national sideshow. But it
was that very dream that derailed the talented, charismatic
young politician who had once shown such promise.

The son of a Serbian immigrant, Rod Blagojevich had
risen far above his humble origins to become the governor of the nation's fifth-largest state, only to see his career
come tumbling down around him. His life in politics had
been launched by his father-in-law, Richard Mell, a savvy,
old-school Chicago alderman who knew how to build
an organization and bring voters to the polls on election
day. But by the time Blagojevich became governor he had
dumped his father-in-law, preferring the counsel of those
who would further and fund his national ambitions.

Blagojevich was building his political power at the same time another young Illinois Democrat was rising through the ranks and making his name known on the national scene. Barack Obama was able to navigate his way through the long history of political corruption in Illinois while Rod Blagojevich was caught up in corrupt schemes seemingly far worse than his predecessors had ever attempted.

The corruption in the Blagojevich administration appeared to take hold from the moment he announced his candidacy for governor in 2001. Those closest to him developed schemes to enrich themselves and the governor's campaign fund by corrupting the hiring process for state positions in agencies and on boards. That the corruption began at the top became clear when Rod Blagojevich was caught on secret government wiretaps talking about "selling" President-elect Obama's vacant Senate seat. "I've got this thing and it's fucking golden and I'm not going to give it up for fucking nothing," Blagojevich tells his top political adviser.

This book is an attempt to tell the story of how Rod Blagojevich's personal biography and political upbringing paved the way for his reckless fall. Although Blagojevich loved politics, he did not like governing. He failed to develop the political relationships with Democrats or Republicans that could have provided him with political cover when the question of impeachment arose. Instead the governor, who had always envisioned himself a populist, turned to the people via the national media. He won good ratings for David Letterman when he appeared on his show, but the vote to impeach and remove him from office was 59 to 0.

Acknowledgments

LATE LAST YEAR I was starting on a Christmas shopping list when I received a phone call from a publisher whose company I was familiar with but whom I had never met. "I'm Ivan Dee," the caller said, "and I'd like to meet with you about a project." What can it be, I wondered, as I walked into Valois, the most famous restaurant/meeting place in Chicago's Hyde Park neighborhood, thanks to the fact that President Barack Obama was a regular breakfast customer not so long ago. "I'd like you to write a book about Rod Blagojevich," Ivan said.

I was flabbergasted. I've been a reporter in Chicago for more than thirty years and have always loved covering the town's politics—the characters, the deals, the accomplishments, the corruption. What other town could produce Barack Obama and Rod Blagojevich at the same time? But I had never contemplated writing a book about what I covered every day.

I had to admit that the rise and fall of Rod Blagojevich was a pretty spectacular story. I had done an early profile of Blagojevich when he first ran for governor in 2002. Afterward I followed him through triumphs and tragedies as he became one more Illinois politician singed by the twin evils of ambition and greed. So I agreed to write my first book. WTTW graciously gave me leave, and I sat down at my computer from six in the morning until ten in the evening every day—except the days when I got stuck. Then I would take a break, go out for a run, and come back and write until 3 a.m.

It never would have happened without the help of my extraordinary researcher Vicki Weger, who provided facts and encouragement at all hours of the day and night. Or without the work of my stepdaughter, Lisa Nuzzo, who turned around transcripts of my interviews with incredible speed and accuracy. Many thanks to Mary Field at WTTW and to Linda Winslow and Patti Parson at *The NewsHour with Jim Lehrer* who gave me the time and encouragement I needed, and to my colleagues in both shops whose workload increased while I worked at the keyboard. Jay Smith was especially helpful with his careful reading of the manuscript. A special thanks to Ivan Dee whose careful editing turned my writing into a book.

I have relied on the reporting of the tenacious and talented Chicago press corps and its coverage of the Blagojevich story, especially the *Chicago Sun-Times* columnists Mark Brown and Carol Marin, whose sharp and pithy analysis is always insightful and accurate. Carol Felsenthal's work in *Chicago* magazine was also extremely helpful.

Thanks to Marc and Sandy McSweeney who graciously allowed me to turn a ski vacation in their beauti-

Acknowledgments

ful mountain home into a writer's retreat. Finally, a huge thank you to my children and grandchildren who were completely ignored while this book took shape. And that goes double for my husband, Peter Martinez. Without his patience, understanding, and support, the book never would have been realized.

E. B.

Chicago
March 2009

Pay to Play

1

The Call

DECEMBER 9, 2008. The ringing phone broke the dark morning's stillness in the Chicago home of the governor of Illinois. Rod Blagojevich, sound asleep, was jolted awake by the call and then the voice on the other end of the line. He would remember the words for the rest of his life.

"There are federal agents at your door waiting to arrest you," said Robert Grant, special agent in charge of the Chicago FBI office.

Stunned, the governor asked, "Is this a joke?" It was not.

His wife, Patti, began to stir. He and Patti had been through a lot together since his election as the fortieth governor of Illinois in 2002. She had defended him fiercely as accusations about "selling" state jobs in exchange for campaign contributions began to swirl around him only months after he took office. She had become estranged from her father, Richard Mell, a powerful Chicago alderman who had single-handedly launched her husband's political career. The break between father and daughter came early on when Mell—perhaps in a battle of egos over real power in the governor's office—accused his son-in-law of "pay to play" politics.

As federal agents entered their home, the two Blagojevich daughters, twelve-year-old Amy and five-year-old Anne, were sound asleep down the hall. The Blagojeviches doted on their daughters. Politics had dominated the girls' lives—Anne was born shortly after her father became governor, and Amy was only two when he won his first political office. Their parents tried to give their girls an ordinary upbringing in the midst of political life. It was a chief reason why Rod had never moved his family into the governor's mansion in Springfield. He, and especially Patti, wanted to raise Amy and Anne in the Chicago neighborhood where Patti had grown up. Their yellow brick home on a corner lot is a little bigger than the other bungalows nearby, but it is far from ostentatious. It sits on a tree-lined street near the north branch of the Chicago River in an area on the northwest side of Chicago known as Ravenswood Manor, which is considered to be far more family friendly than many other Chicago neighborhoods. They liked the girls' school where Patti had always been an involved parent. Their decision not to move to Springfield, the capital city, had irked legislators and set an early tone for the governor's combative relationship with lawmakers.

Now, while his children slept, Blagojevich put on the black-and-blue jogging suit he liked for his daily run through the neighborhood and went to face the FBI. The arrest had come in the very early morning hours in an FBI effort to spare the children the trauma of seeing their father taken from their home. "All the people involved in this investigation are parents," Robert Grant said. "We are always sensitive to people's personal situations and, when we can control it, we try to never embarrass anyone regardless of their alleged crime."

But according to several reports, Blagojevich began acting strangely when he confronted the agents. The governor commenced a series of stretching exercises, started jogging in place—and then stunned agents by lying down in the fetal position. He went through this strange routine several times without saying a word.

By this time Patti was awake and with her husband when, as part of standard FBI procedure, he was handcuffed and led out of their home into the cold December morning—their hopes and dreams of a successful political career as governor and maybe even a future run for the presidency of the United States going out the door with him.

The governor was driven downtown to the sleek Federal Center, one of Chicago's iconic loop landmarks, designed by Mies van der Rohe. He could have been taken to the grim Metropolitan Correctional Center, the federal jail known as the MCC; but the two arresting agents held him along with his chief of staff, John Harris, also arrested that morning, in a small room near the federal courtrooms. The governor sat silently, appearing to be almost in shock after the morning's events. He called his lawyer, an old friend Sheldon Sorosky, who had given Blagojevich one of his first jobs out of law school years before. Six hours later, still dressed in his jogging suit, Rod Blagojevich stood before U.S. Magistrate Judge Jan Nolan in the formal courtroom on the eighteenth floor of the Dirksen Building.

Senator Everett McKinley Dirksen, Republican from Illinois, had been known for his support of key civil rights legislation in the 1960s as well as his strong sense of ethics. The man who stood in the courtroom of the Dirksen Building, listening to the reading of the charges brought against him, seemed to descend from a different line of Illinois politicians—the long lineage of those engaged in political corruption. But even considering the sad litany of corrupt politicians who had come before him, the charges against Illinois governor Rod Blagojevich were stunning, including his attempt to "sell" the U.S. Senate seat of President-elect Barack Obama.

As governor, Blagojevich had the sole authority to appoint Obama's replacement. The federal government had wiretapped many of the governor's telephone conversations over previous months and caught Blagojevich on tape expressing an unwillingness to hand over the Senate seat without anything in return. Transcripts of the tapes presented to the federal judge quoted the governor as saying that the Senate seat ". . . is a fucking valuable thing, you just don't give it away for nothing." And in another taped conversation, ". . . I've got this thing and it's fucking golden, and, uh, uh, I'm just not giving it up for fucking nothing. I'm not gonna do it. And I can always use it. I can parachute me in there."

Those charges were just the tip of the swill. The government was also charging Blagojevich with trying to have the editorial writers of the *Chicago Tribune* fired for going after his administration, and for parceling out state jobs and contracts in exchange for campaign contributions—what's known in Illinois as classic "pay to play" politics.

Blagojevich folded his arms in front of him and listened to the charges being read. When the hearing ended, the governor, appearing unshaken, walked over to Assistant U.S. Attorney Carrie Hamilton, spoke to her, and shook her hand, a highly unusual gesture.

U.S. Attorney Patrick Fitzgerald had carefully orchestrated the case against Governor Blagojevich. Since arriving in Chicago on September 1, 2001, just ten days before 9/11, Fitzgerald's fights against political corruption had reached legendary proportions. Not long after his appointment, headline writers began calling Fitzgerald a modern-day Eliot Ness. Ness had been called into Chicago eighty years earlier to clean up a crime spree led by the country's most notorious mobster, Al Capone. At the press conference following the arrest of Blagojevich, Fitzgerald called the governor's actions in the weeks before he was taken into custody "a political corruption crime spree." The incorruptible Ness had been known as an "untouchable" for his ability to stay on the straight and narrow while pursuing the country's most dangerous criminals.

The privilege of recommending the United States Attorney for the Northern District of Illinois goes to the state's senior senator of the same party as the president. At the time of Fitzgerald's appointment, that was another Fitzgerald, Peter—no relation to Patrick. Peter was an independent Republican who won a seat in the Senate after defeating Illinois' first African-American senator, Carol Moseley Braun. An "untouchable" crime fighter was exactly the kind of prosecutor he was looking for when the time came to fill the job of U.S. attorney. Little else will be remembered from Senator Peter Fitzgerald's one term in the U.S. Senate from 1999 to 2005. But his choice of U.S. Attorney Patrick Fitzgerald left an indelible mark on the State of Illinois.

Peter Fitzgerald won his Senate race with little help from the regular Republican organization, led at that time by Governor George Ryan. Senator Fitzgerald and Governor Ryan tangled repeatedly over Illinois issues, and it was clear to everyone that Senator Fitzgerald was not a team player. Ryan was already under federal investigation for political corruption when Peter Fitzgerald was elected to the Senate.

When Senator Fitzgerald decided not to run for reelection in 2004, a couple of major events ensued. First, his decision paved the way for an eventual win by Barack Obama. Second, the senator wanted to make sure the federal investigations already under way into political corruption in Illinois would continue. In 2005 he told me, "The allies of the governor were pressuring me to put someone in office who would see things more favorably for the governor, and so I was very concerned that whoever I recommended as U.S. attorney be someone who was totally independent. And in finding Patrick Fitzgerald I found someone of unquestioned independence and integrity and truly top-notch ability."

Patrick Fitzgerald was an unusual choice. The son of Irish immigrants, he had grown up in Brooklyn with no ties at all to Chicago. His father worked as a doorman in an upscale coop building on East Seventy-fifth Street in Manhattan. Like Rod Blagojevich's hardworking immigrant parents, they stressed the value of education to their son. Patrick won a scholarship to Regis, a prestigious Jesuit high school. In the summers, to earn money for college, he worked as a janitor in a Manhattan apartment building just down the street from his father's job.

With the help of scholarships, summer jobs, and part-time work, Patrick made it to Amherst College in Massachusetts, one of the top five liberal arts colleges in the country, and surprised no one by graduating Phi Beta Kappa. He went on to Harvard Law School, graduating in 1985. Tall and athletic, Patrick Fitzgerald never played conventional sports, but he did join the rugby team at Harvard and kept up that hardscrabble sport well into his twenties. He told a *New York Times* reporter he enjoyed rugby because "You get every stress out of your system. You kick the ball, tackle, and are tackled. At the end of the game, there's no unspent energy left."

Fitzgerald began his prosecutorial career as an assistant U.S. attorney in the Southern District of New York. He spent thirteen years there and earned a reputation as a thorough, relentless prosecutor with a legendary work ethic, often driving himself into the wee hours of the morning while others slept. An often-repeated story has a police officer coming into Fitzgerald's decidedly bachelor apartment in Brooklyn and noticing papers piled on top of his gas stove. "Don't worry about a problem with fire," Fitzgerald told him, "I've never turned it on."

In his first big case, Patrick Fitzgerald sent New York mobster John Gambino to federal prison. He also went after followers of a relatively unknown Middle Eastern terrorist and convicted four of his associates for the 1998 bombings of U.S. embassies. That was before Osama bin Laden became a household name. Fitzgerald had already put five defendants behind bars in connection with the 1993 World Trade Center bombings. No wonder the staff of the 9/11 Commission called him one of the world's best terrorism prosecutors.

For a man compelled to root out official corruption, the offer to come to Chicago must have been almost irresistible. Although he knew no one in the city, it was clear to Fitzgerald that there would be plenty to do for even the most work-obsessed prosecutor.

Historically in Chicago, the U.S. attorney's office had a tinge of patronage in the appointment process and had been used by many appointees as a stepping-stone to higher office. The late Chicago mayor Richard J. Daley (father of the current mayor) would frequently remind those in the legendary Chicago political machine that the U.S. attorney's office was one of the three most important offices in the state and that no mayor or governor should ever feel comfortable when the U. S. attorney was from the opposing political party.

Patrick Fitzgerald was perhaps exactly the kind of U.S. attorney the senior Mayor Daley was talking about. Without a hint of politics or patronage in Patrick Fitzgerald's office, he soon had politicians from both parties quaking when they feared he was sniffing around their bailiwicks. Dean Polales worked in the U.S. attorney's office with Fitzgerald during his first three years in Chicago and confirms that as a crime fighter Fitzgerald is completely apolitical: "I don't think Democratic or Republican party politics has anything to do with the way he does his job. And I think his track record in Chicago demonstrates that . . . when dealing with political corruption cases, he's an equal-opportunity prosecutor."

One of Fitzgerald's most important cases occurred two years after he arrived in Chicago, and it had nothing to do with Illinois or Chicago politics. He was appointed special counsel to investigate the leak that exposed Valerie Plame as a CIA agent after her husband, Joseph Wilson, was sent to Africa to investigate reports that Iraq was importing uranium from Niger. In the course of the investigation, Fitzgerald jailed *New York Times* reporter Judith Miller for contempt of court for failing to reveal her sources and threatened to jail *Time* magazine reporter Matt Cooper. The action outraged editors at the *Times* and many other journalists. The *Times* editorial page blasted Fitzgerald, charging that "in his zeal to compel reporters to disclose their sources, Mr. Fitzgerald lost sight of the bigger picture." The paper called the case "a major assault" on relationships between reporters and their secret sources, a necessary weapon in reporting on the abuse of power.

Even some Democrats thought Fitzgerald had gone too far. David Axelrod, the political consultant who led Barack Obama's presidential campaign to victory, told me in 2003 that Fitzgerald's pursuit of Judith Miller in the Plame case pointed up the man's shortcomings. "This is a guy who spent his life in the prosecutor's office, never really lived and worked elsewhere, and he sees the world in very stark terms—good and evil, black and white," Axelrod said. "There's never any grey in Patrick Fitzgerald's world. And so he goes after people—indiscriminately, in my view—whether large or small, and uses very broad interpretations of the law to do it because he thinks that's the right thing to do."

Fitzgerald made no apologies for his vigorous prosecution in the Plame case, telling the *New York Times*, ". . . as a prosecutor you have two roles: Show judgment as to what to go after and how to go after it. But also once you do that, be zealous. And if you're not zealous, you shouldn't have the job. Now sometimes zealous becomes a code word for overzealous and I don't want to be overzealous. I hope I'm not." Fitzgerald eventually won a conviction of Lewis "Scooter" Libby, Vice President Cheney's chief of staff—not for leaking Valerie Plame's name but for lying to federal investigators about the leak. President George W. Bush subsequently commuted Libby's sentence on July 2, 2007.

Back in Chicago after the Libby conviction, Patrick Fitzgerald took up where he had left off—meticulously examining the persistent culture of political corruption in Illinois.

2

A Tradition of Corruption

"IF ILLINOIS isn't the most corrupt state in the United States, it's certainly one hell of a competitor." The FBI's Robert Grant hurled those words into the atmosphere at the press conference following the arrest of Governor Blagojevich. While it may have made some Illinois politicos wince, the FBI chief didn't receive much argument from them. Illinoisans have a long love/hate relationship with their state's reputation for producing scoundrels and scallywags. The colorful characters who dot the state's political landscape are part and parcel of the state's raucous, brawling identity, particularly in the city of Chicago.

The antics of Mike "Hinky Dink" Kenna and "Bathhouse John" Coughlin, two bosses who ruled Chicago's First Ward from the late nineteenth century until World War II, are legendary. The ward, which later became much of what is now known as "The Loop" in downtown Chicago was one of the most infamous havens for vice in the entire United States, home to magnificent gambling palaces, ornate houses of prostitution, and saloons, bars, and dives of immense variety. "Hinky Dink" was the brains behind the operation while the gregarious "Bathhouse John" was the front man. As Democrats, the two men controlled the party and its coffers, and both served as alderman of the First Ward. They immediately sold protection to the ward's pimps, prostitutes, and gamblers, which included lawyers who would be on the spot if arrests came. In exchange Kenna and Coughlin received a cut of the proceeds from the illegal activities. Each year they sent out elaborate invitations to the magnificent First Ward Ball, a political fund-raiser that no prostitute, burglar, politician, businessman, safecracker, or saloon keeper dared to turn down when the ticket sellers came around. The ball brought in an annual $50,000 a year and nearly always ended with the patrons, dressed in their jewels, feathers, and furs, rioting in the streets. The outrageous corruption led to the founding of the first reform organization in the city, the Civic Federation, which still exists today.

In the 1970s a political reform group dedicated to "electing independent and honest politicians"—the Independent Precinct Organization—revived the First Ward Ball as its major fund-raiser, proving once again that Chicagoans' fascination with their corrupt politicians is a source of perverse pride and mischievous entertainment.

Corruption got an early start too in the state capital in Springfield. Governor Joel Aldrich Matteson (1853–1857) tried to cash in $200,000 in government script, explaining that he had "found" it in a shoebox. A judge bought the governor's explanation that he had no idea how the script had made its way into the shoebox. The judge agreed not to accept an indictment if the governor turned the money over to the state.

Another Illinois governor escaped indictment in the 1920s despite substantial evidence that he had embezzled more than $1 million in state funds while in office. Governor Lennington Small went on to serve seven more years in office.

And though he was never governor, Illinois Secretary of State Paul Powell appears to have gotten away with fleecing the taxpayers out of more money than anyone before him. Powell, who was elected to the office in 1964 and again in 1968, had a simple definition of political success: "There's only one thing worse than a defeated politician, and that's a broke one." Powell was never defeated and, as it turned out at his death, he was not broke either. The highest office Powell ever held was secretary of state, and the highest salary he ever received was $30,000 a year. Yet after a lifetime of public service, when Paul Powell died in 1970 at the age of sixty-eight he left an estate that exceeded $3 million. Police officers gathering up his belongings from the Springfield hotel suite where he had been living did not believe anything suspicious had occurred until they came across $800,000, *in cash,* stuffed in shoeboxes, briefcases, and strongboxes in the closet. Upon investigation they realized that when Illinois residents came to the secretary of state's office to renew their driver's license and were told to write out their checks simply to "Paul Powell," at least part of the money really did go to Paul Powell. Taxpayers were both aghast and amused by the idea of Powell stuffing hundreds of thousands of dollars into shoeboxes, all the while continuing his modest way of life.

Powell was emblematic of the Illinois politicians who built their political organizations—and apparently their personal fortunes—on patronage. In his role as secretary of state, Powell had more than two thousand jobs to hand out. He understood and wielded the power those jobs gave him. Whenever the subject of state jobs came up, he was known to say, "I can smell the meat a-cookin'." Those who were awarded jobs were expected to give back, perhaps by working for Powell's election and re-elections, or contributing to his campaigns, or both. This was the "pay-to-play" politics of its day, which at the time no one saw as corrupt. It was simply the "way things worked" in Illinois.

Political corruption in the state had its roots in the momentous population movements of the nineteenth century. As Irish, Germans, Poles, and others came to Illinois, jobs were hard to come by. The new immigrants faced intense discrimination and grew to realize they would have to organize themselves politically in order to gain power. As their political organizations gained strength and began taking control of precincts, then wards, and finally city and state governments, immigrant politicians built these organizations by handing out jobs. Once a new immigrant had a job, walking a precinct for a candidate or a political party seemed like a small price to pay for holding on to that job. It wasn't long before working a precinct became a requirement for getting a job, enabling these political organizations to gain more and more control over who would work in state and local government.

Richard J. Daley, the legendary boss of Chicago, took over the Cook County Democratic party when he became mayor in 1955 and proceeded to build the nation's strongest political machine. Daley's predecessor, Martin J. Kennelly, had been seen as an ineffectual reformer. So it was, on the election night when Richard J. Daley took the throne, that Alderman Paddy Bauler danced a jig and belted out his now-famous words, "Chicago ain't ready for reform!" Over the next twenty-one years, Daley's machine delivered again and again in providing city services and in getting out votes for the Democratic party. Handing out city jobs in exchange for precinct work or political contributions was never seen as corruption. Rather, it was seen as a means of providing "good government and good politics," as the mayor liked to say.

The colorful antics and continuing corruption of many politicians made fertile ground for strong reformers in Chicago. They worked particularly hard to try to break the power of Daley's Democratic machine. After Daley's election to office, no one had any doubts about who was running Chicago. Reformers set out to make Daley more responsive to the citizenry.

The same year Mayor Daley was elected mayor, Leon Despres was voted in as Fifth Ward alderman. Despres represented the South Side's Hyde Park neighborhood, which had enjoyed its heyday during the 1893 World's Columbian Exposition in Chicago. It is a sprawling and sometimes grand area of mansions, museums, and ordinary apartment buildings along the gorgeous lakefront of Lake Michigan. It is also famously home to the University of Chicago, politically progressive, and still one of the only solidly integrated neighborhoods in the city, the neighborhood where Barack Obama began his political career and where he has a home. Alderman Despres spent his twenty-year career on the City Council railing against the power of "Boss" Daley's political patronage armies and the mayor's opposition to the integration of Chicago's neighborhoods and schools. For his trouble, Despres usually found that his microphone was cut off during City Council debates and that he was on the losing end of many 49-to-1 votes. In 1972 the acerbic Chicago newspaper columnist Mike Royko described Despres' career this way: "He has been in the forefront of just about every decent, worthwhile effort made to improve life in this city. Being in the forefront, he is usually the first to be hit on the head with the mayor's gavel."

Another alderman joined Despres in his lonely fight against the Democratic machine. In 1969 Bill Singer beat the machine candidate in Paddy Bauler's old Forty-third Ward. Six years later Singer went on to run for mayor against Daley. Despite building his own precinct operation and raising more money than anyone ever had in a run against the boss, Daley won in a landslide with 77 percent of the vote. Indeed, Chicago still wasn't ready for reform.

Richard J. Daley never ran afoul of the law because of personal or political corruption. Most Chicagoans believed he was a personally honest man. But plenty of those around him got caught with their hands in the city's coffers. Thomas Keane, Daley's longtime floor leader in the City Council, was convicted and served prison time for federal wire fraud and for making millions of dollars on secret land deals. The day after Keane's conviction, his law partner, Alderman Paul Wigoda, was convicted for income tax evasion on a $50,000 bribe he'd taken from a real estate developer for pushing a zoning change through the City Council. And the day after that Daley's former press secretary, Earl Bush, went down on eleven counts of federal mail fraud. It marked the beginning of the end of America's last great political machine.

One Chicago political reformer who was never elected to public office had a major impact on changing the way politics is played in Chicago. In 1969 twenty-nine-year-old Chicago lawyer Michael Shakman filed a lawsuit against the Democratic Organization of Cook County, Illinois. He argued that political patronage is illegal because it places nonpolitical candidates and job seekers at an unconstitutional disadvantage. It took a lot of years and many rulings to move the case through the courts, but by 1983 it finally became illegal to consider political factors when hiring or firing public employees, unless they worked in top administrative or policymaking positions.

After the so-called Shakman Decrees, political leaders from Mayor Richard J. Daley to his son, Mayor Richard M. Daley, to Governor Rod Blagojevich, never stopped looking for ways around the court's decision against patronage. Illinois politicians were genuinely stunned when the feds came after them for hiring or firing for political reasons. While the political landscape was finally beginning to change in Illinois, those in power were slow to notice the shift.

One of those caught up in the crosswinds of the changing political culture was U.S. Congressman Dan Rostenkowski. He had begun his political career as a pure product of Richard J. Daley's Cook County Democratic machine. Rostenkowski would have run for alderman, the usual entry-level position for machine candidates, but that post was already held by his father, Joseph, a tough alderman and ward boss of the largely Polish-American Thirty-second Ward on the northwest side, who had held the job for twenty-four years. Joe had helped elect Mayor Daley, and when it was time for Rostenkowski's son,

Danny, to join the family's political business, the Thirty-second Ward's Democratic precinct captains put the word out on the streets for voters to support the alderman's son. Thus the son became Illinois State Representative Dan Rostenkowski. Nine years later, in 1958, he was elected to Congress, representing the interests of Chicagoans and, more important, the concerns of Daley's Democratic political machine. Years later Rod Blagojevich would win the same congressional seat Rostenkowski once held.

For thirty-six years Rostenkowski worked the halls of Congress, building a reputation as one of the most skillful politicians of his day. He crafted important and successful legislation and never forgot to bring home the bacon for Chicago. Reporters sometimes referred to him as the "Prince of Pork." As the powerful chairman of the House Ways and Means Committee from 1981 to 1994, he played an important role in tax and trade policy.

Rostenkowski played politics the Chicago way. And in 1994 that got him into trouble. He was arrested and faced seventeen counts in a federal indictment for misusing the powers of his office. Some of the charges included larding his office staff with patronage workers who failed to show up for work—commonly called "ghost employees." The indictment also charged him with using congressional funds to buy gifts such as chairs and ashtrays for friends, and trading in stamps for cash at the House post office.

Before the indictment was filed, government prosecutors offered Rostenkowski a chance to resign from Congress, plead guilty to one count, and serve six months in prison. He responded, ". . . Truth is on my side," adding, "I will not make any deals with them. I did not commit any crimes."

The words were similar to and the sentiment exactly the same as the declarations of Governor Rod Blagojevich fourteen years later as he faced reporters in his first press conference after his arrest on criminal charges. "I will fight. I will fight. I will fight until I take my last breath," the governor said over the sound of cameras snapping like machine-gun fire. "I have done nothing wrong."

But the political playing field had shifted under Dan Rostenkowski's feet. Things he had done for years—finding jobs for family and friends who had worked in his campaigns, handing out gifts to supporters, using the House post office as a bank when he was short of cash—were suddenly illegal. Rostenkowski truly never *got it* and persisted in thinking he had done nothing wrong. But the federal court disagreed. Two years later, when he finally stopped fighting and pled guilty to reduced charges of mail fraud, he was sentenced to seventeen months in prison. He served fifteen months and never really admitted to any wrongdoing. When he was transferred to prison, he could not bear for his wife and daughters to see him incarcerated and actually forbade them to visit him for more than a year.

With so many Chicago politicians before him taken down by federal prosecutors, Rod Blagojevich had to know the rules had changed. But somehow he seemed to think those changes did not apply to *him*. Federal prosecutors and the FBI were amazed—and angered—by Blagojevich's brazenness in the wake of the convictions of politicians who preceded him. On the day of the governor's arrest, the FBI's Robert Grant told reporters, "Many, including myself, thought that the recent convictions of a former governor [George Ryan] would usher in a new era of honesty and reform in Illinois politics.

Clearly the charges announced today reveal that the Office of Governor has become nothing more than a vehicle for self–enrichment, unrestricted by party affiliation, and taking Illinois politics to a new low."

The low road of Illinois politics had been well-traveled by previous governors. Three of the seven who served before Blagojevich were convicted and served serious jail time.

Democratic governor Otto Kerner, a tall, handsome man, had a perfect profile for politics: a graduate of Brown University, law degree from Northwestern, married to a former Chicago mayor's daughter, Bronze Star for service in World War II. Elected in 1960 and 1964, Governor Kerner served without a hint of scandal. Appointed to the U.S. Court of Appeals in 1968, he resigned in disgrace in 1974 after he was convicted on seventeen counts of bribery and related charges. The manager of two Illinois racetracks had given then Governor Kerner $356,000 worth of stock in her horse-racing operation. In exchange the governor had arranged for her track to have the best racing dates of the season. Kerner was sentenced to three years in prison but was diagnosed with terminal cancer and released after serving eight months. Such were the circumstances of dealings with Illinois public officials that Marge Lindheimer Everett, the tracks manager, actually believed the bribe was a legitimate, federally deductible expense for doing business with the state.

Horse racing has long been a magnet for corruption in Illinois. One of the charges against Blagojevich in the federal criminal complaint accuses him of demanding a campaign contribution before signing a bill that would direct a percentage of casino revenues to the horse-racing industry.

After Otto Kerner, the next governor to wind up behind bars was Dan Walker, a Democrat who ran as a reformer against Daley's Democratic machine. Without the benefit of the Democratic organization to turn out the vote for him, Dan Walker set out to *walk* across Illinois, a distance of 1,197 miles, wearing his signature red bandana, work shirt, and jeans in order to relate to everyday voters. His stunt caught the imagination of the media—and Illinois voters—and Dan Walker won a single term as governor, from 1973 to 1977. But it wasn't easy.

Walker had hoped for cooperation from the Illinois legislature, but in his autobiography, *The Maverick and the Machine*, he describes the confrontational relationship that developed. "Right out of the box, my own party leaders deserted me and refused to confirm my Cabinet appointees. In effect, they spit in my face, and the Republicans kicked me in the ass. But what are you going to do? Lay down, or fight them? So I fought them." When the Democrats won majorities in both houses of the legislature during the last two years of Walker's administration, he was able to bring some reform to the state with new ethics legislation and tighter laws regarding political patronage.

Like Blagojevich, Walker had dreams of running for President of the United States, but when he lost in the primary in the race for his second term those dreams evaporated. Rod Blagojevich found himself in similar fights with the Illinois legislature, crippling the operation of state government for most of his governorship.

Like former Governor Kerner, Dan Walker's legal troubles began after he left office when he was convicted for obtaining fraudulent loans for his business and personal use from a savings and loan bank that he owned. At his sentencing, U.S. District Judge Ann Williams told him, "It's clear to this court that a pattern was established and that you, Mr. Walker, thought this bank was your own personal piggy bank to bail you out whenever you got into trouble." He was sentenced to seven years and served eighteen months at a Duluth, Minnesota, federal prison.

In 2001, when Patrick Fitzgerald arrived in Chicago, political corruption trials reached a new level. Fitzgerald went after city, county, and state politicians with an aggresiveness never before seen from the U.S. attorney's office. One of the sacred cows he took on was the political patronage system in the city of Chicago. Richard M. Daley had been mayor for twelve years and held firm control of the city's political operations when Fitzgerald took over as U.S. attorney. The city had flourished in many ways under Daley's leadership, and he credited the professional managers and staff he had placed in key departments for the city's success. Revamping the city's schools under the leadership of his appointee Paul Vallas was the mayor's toughest challenge, and he touted the important progress Vallas made. Neighborhoods were revitalized across the city, helped by good economic times and a well-run city Department of Planning—led at one point by Valerie Jarrett, currently one of President Barack Obama's chief advisers. Where his father had been the "Boss," Daley frequently referred to himself as the city's "CEO." He did not take the job as chairman of the Cook County Democratic party, as his father had, and he often said that the Democratic machine and the old patronage system were long gone. Nonetheless, through his corporation counsel young Daley challenged the Shakman Decrees, alleging that they "interfered with the smooth operation of city government and were no longer needed."

It was an imaginative effort, but the argument came to a screeching halt on July 18, 2005, when Patrick Fitzgerald brought federal charges against leading city officials in Daley's administration for "violating the Shakman Decrees against the political hiring and firing of city employees." In a news conference announcing the charges, Fitzgerald reiterated that "Every resident of Chicago has the right to compete fairly for a job if he or she is qualified, without regard to political affiliation or whether they do campaign work. Every applicant who sits for an interview is entitled to an honest evaluation. And the residents of Chicago are entitled to the best-qualified laborers, plumbers, foremen, and inspectors. And when a federal court order requires that people be hired or promoted without regard to political affiliation, the court order must be followed. Yet, for a decade, certifications by city officials that the law has been complied with have often been fraudulent. Qualified persons sat for interviews for jobs that had already been doled out as a reward for political work. The defendants are charged with a pervasive fraud scheme that included fixing applicant interviews and ratings, guaranteeing that preferred job candidates would be chosen over other equally or better-suited individuals, and then falsifying personnel documents to conceal their wrongdoing." He added, "The diversion of public resources to benefit political organizations, by using fraudulently obtained jobs and promotions as currency to compensate political workers, cheats the city and its employees, and improperly advantages those political organizations with influential government sponsors."

Three of the four city officials eventually charged came from the mayor's old Bridgeport neighborhood where he had grown up and where the legendary Eleventh Ward political organization was based. Robert Sorich, a soft-spoken, slightly built man who was forty-three at the time of his trial, had worked as an aide to the Eleventh Ward alderman and often shared rides to work with Mayor Richard M. Daley's brother John, a Cook County commissioner. Sorich's father had been the official photographer for Richard J. Daley. A second defendant, Patrick Slattery, lived on the same Bridgeport block as John Daley, and his wife had been a secretary in the mayor's office. Like Sorich, Timothy McCarthy had worked as an aide to the Eleventh Ward alderman, and his father had worked for Richard M. Daley before he was mayor, when he was Cook County state's attorney.

Fitzgerald's criminal charges shocked many of the city's politicians. In the past, violations of the Shakman Decrees had been treated as civil, not criminal, matters. Sorich's defense attorney argued that the government was stretching the law beyond the breaking point by criminalizing political hiring. Longtime Chicago alderman Bernard Stone told me that Patrick Fitzgerald had gone too far. "Nobody has ever dealt with it on a criminal basis," Stone said. "The only one who's ever called it a criminal matter is this current U.S. attorney. Either we're a country of laws or we're a country where the U.S. attorney decides that we are what he says we are."

South Side alderman William Beavers was equally upset with Fitzgerald: "I think he's trying to dictate to city hall how to do hiring. The federal government hires on the patronage system. The city should hire on the patronage system. There's nothing wrong with recommending somebody." Beavers's reputation as a political powerhouse came in great part from political patronage.

Although Daley continued to deny the existence of a patronage system under his administration, many of those who worked for him believed it to be unfathomable that the city could function efficiently without political patronage. What kind of control would elected officials have over city employees if they had not had a hand in the hiring of those employees? How could political organizations be built to support the mayor and his candidates without the ability to offer city jobs and promotions in return? It was the way of political life in Chicago.

In July 2006 Fitzgerald's prosecutors sent a new and different message to the Chicago political world when they won convictions in the political patronage case. Robert Sorich was sentenced to forty-six months in prison. His Bridgeport neighbors who had packed the courtroom were stunned. Tears welled up in Sorich's eyes, and his wife burst into sobs. Days later, Mayor Daley defended Sorich and his three co-defendants, all of whom were convicted. "I know all those young men personally, and their families," the mayor said, "and they are very fine young men, and their families."

A year later the Daley administration continued to insist that patronage no longer existed in the city but agreed to settle the decades-old Shakman case and establish a $12 million fund to compensate victims of illegal political discrimination.

Classical patronage—trading jobs for political favors—was not the only kind of patronage in the Daley administration. Much more prevalent was so-called pinstripe patronage, the doling out of millions of dollars in contracts to clout-heavy friends who usually responded with fat political contributions. Stung by charges that pinstripe patronage had dominated his administration since his election in 1989, Daley in March 2005 called for a ban on contributions to his mayoral campaign from city contractors.

Governor Blagojevich and his minions had no appetite for the same ban on contractor contributions at the state level. Those who did business with the state had long been the largest source of campaign funds for governors and state legislators. That fund-raising practice—in itself perfectly legal, but not if it became a payment for favors—gave Patrick Fitzgerald plenty of material when he brought his biggest case of political corruption to trial against Blagojevich's predecessor, Governor George Ryan. "Operation Safe Roads," the federal investigation into political corruption in the administrations of George Ryan, both as governor and as Illinois secretary of state, began in September 1998. That was during the term of U.S. Attorney Scott Lassar, three years before Fitzgerald came to town and two months before Ryan was elected to his first term as governor on the Republican ticket.

George Ryan cultivated his reputation as a cigar-chomping, old-school politician who liked to make deals. He made no apologies for wielding his clout in the service of his friends—those who helped him were awarded state jobs and state contracts. His ability to work both sides of the aisle in Springfield, with fellow Republicans and with Democrats, enabled Ryan in 1999 to pass the largest public works program in the state's history, a $6.3 billion package to repair the state's infrastructure. The new legislation also contained plenty of state contracts to be passed around.

Governor Ryan gained national attention in 2000 when he declared a moratorium on the state's death penalty, responding to repeated revelations of innocent men on death row. Many of the cases had been investigated and overturned by students at Northwestern University. "There is a flaw in the system, without question, and it needs to be studied. I want to make sure . . . that the person who is put to death is absolutely guilty," Ryan said. His decision to call the moratorium was seen as courageous by many, especially coming from a Republican governor, and it earned him nominations for the Nobel Peace Prize in 2005, 2006, 2007, and 2008.

But charges of corruption during his tenure as secretary of state began to dog him in his first campaign for governor. In their Operation Safe Roads investigation, the feds charged that under a scheme inside the secretary of state's office, unqualified truck drivers paid bribes to obtain their driver's licenses, and that money then found its way into George Ryan's campaign funds. Candidate Ryan denied knowledge of the scheme. The investigation might never have escalated had it not been for a horrific and deadly crash on a Wisconsin expressway that killed the six young children of Scott and Janet Willis on election day 1994. The driver of the truck that caused the Willises' van to crash and explode into flames was an unqualified driver who had paid a bribe for his license.

For the next three years the U.S. attorney's office pursued the case against Ryan, working its way up the food chain of state employees, first in the secretary of state's office and then in the governor's office itself. By the time Fitzgerald took over as U.S. attorney, thirty state employees had been indicted, and almost all had pled guilty and been sentenced. Even as Fitzgerald accelerated the investigation and indictments continued, George Ryan kept right on governing the way he always had—making deals and doling out state contracts to friends in exchange for gifts and loans to himself and his family.

Nearing seventy years of age, George Ryan never thought of himself as corrupt. He felt the same way so many other public officials had over the years—this was the way business and politics were done in Illinois. But as the number of arrests grew and public outrage mounted, the pressure forced George Ryan out of the race for a second term as governor.

Nearly a year after he had left the governor's office, on December 17, 2003, Patrick Fitzgerald announced an eighteen-count indictment against Ryan, charging him with public corruption during his terms of secretary of state and governor. Ryan became the sixty-sixth defendant indicted in the Operation Safe Roads probe. Fitzgerald told reporters that Ryan had put the governor's office up for sale. "The citizens of Illinois have a fundamental right to honest government. They should expect and receive nothing less. The charged conduct by former Governor Ryan reflects a disturbing violation of that trust. . . . By giving friends free rein over state employees and state business to make profits—and by steering those profits to his friends and, at times, his family, defendant Ryan sold his office."

After a six-month trial, at which Ryan mounted a vigorous defense, he was convicted on all eighteen counts. The silver-haired and grandfatherly former governor had endured the long trial with dignity, bowing to his high-priced lawyer's request not to testify in his own defense. But as the verdicts were read, he glared at each juror, his eyes never moving off the jury box as each juror answered "yes" when asked if they agreed with the guilty verdicts. Lura Lynn Ryan, the governor's wife of forty-nine years, who had sat through nearly every day of the trial, looked dazed as she watched her husband's political career come crashing down. Ryan, surrounded by family members, was grim as he left the courtroom, telling the throng of waiting reporters, "I believe this decision today is not in accordance with the kind of public service that I provided to the people of Illinois over 40 years, and needless to say I am disappointed in the outcome."

Just as Dan Rostenkowski and Robert Sorich and others before them had never believed they were guilty of anything beyond politics as usual in Illinois, George Ryan remained adamant that he had done nothing wrong. On his last night of freedom before he began serving his six-and-a-half-year prison sentence, Ryan met reporters on the front lawn of his Kankakee, Illinois, home. It was a dark and cold November evening as Ryan, now seventy-three, huddled closely with his wife and children. Although he was at last defeated, his rhetoric was passionate: "I will report to the federal corrections facility in Oxford, Wisconsin, as ordered . . . but I do so with a clear conscience, and I have said since the beginning of this ten-year ordeal that I'm innocent and I intend to prove it."

But Patrick Fitzgerald offered a completely different assessment of George Ryan's political career. He called the governor's actions "a low-water mark for public service." Fitzgerald could not have known that in just a few more years he would have to admit that he had underestimated just how low Illinois politicians could stoop. At the 2008 news conference announcing criminal charges against George Ryan's successor, Rod Blagojevich, Fitzgerald observed, "This is a sad day for government. Governor Blagojevich has taken us to a truly new low."

3

A Typical American Kid

ROD BLAGOJEVICH's parents did not live long enough to see their younger son's meteoric rise to become governor of the great state of Illinois. Nor did they witness his equally spectacular fall from that high office. Both events would undoubtedly have been more than they could ever have imagined.

Rod's father, Rade Blagojevich, had been born in 1911 in a small village outside of Belgrade, Yugoslovia. He was the son of pig farmers who lived a meager and difficult rural life. It was hard to imagine that things could be worse for the little family, but then World War II arrived. At the age of thirty, Rade and his brother Milorad, for whom the governor is named, joined the army of the Yugoslovian Kingdom, as it was called at the time. They would fight with the Allies against Hitler's armies. In 1941 the brothers were home on leave when Nazis attacked their village. Nazi storm troopers rounded up all the villagers and threatened to kill everyone if any soldiers hiding in the area did not turn themselves in. The two young Blagojevich brothers, both artillery officers, stepped forward in surrender. The Nazis forced them into the back of an army truck for the long ride to the German border. For the next four years Rade and Milorad were held as German prisoners of war, longing for the simple life they had once lived. When the war ended, relatives thought the Blagojevich brothers should start new lives in the land of opportunity, the United States of America. They were directed to contact the Serbian Orthodox Church in Libertyville, Illinois, which had helped resettle other Serbian refugees. When church members heard the story of Rade and Milorad, they arranged to bring the two men to Chicago. Neither spoke a word of English, nor did they have a single dime. But they were willing to work hard and were determined to make a go of it in America.

Four years and much hard work later, Rade Blagojevich met a young woman at a dance sponsored by the neighborhood Serbian Social Club. She caught his eye. Her parents had immigrated to Chicago from Bosnia and Herzegovina. Millie Govedarcia, a vibrant and outgoing woman, worked hard to fit into the American culture; she wanted her life to be everything that was American. But she fell deeply in love with the handsome Serb who was eleven years older, and in 1950 they married. Their first son, Bojidod, was born six years later, and just sixteen months later Milorod was born. Those were the names their father chose for his boys, but Millie wanted her sons to have American names too. She insisted that the name *Robert* be on Bojidod's birth certificate and *Rod* on Milorod's. The names were indicative of the way the boys grew up, straddling both Serbian and American cultures.

Robert Blagojevich gives his mother most of the credit for helping her sons navigate the divide between the two cultures. "My father was very strong in his nationalism," he says. "But my mother was the balancing factor there to keep it all sort of normal. If it were up to my dad, we would be back in Yugoslavia, in the village raising cows, wearing *lubyankas*—Serbian shoes. My mother, knowing we were American and were going to grow up here, still made sure that we honored the nationality and our faith. We spoke Serbian at home, but she made sure that when we were outside the home we were acclimating to the American way of life."

Saving money for the boys' education was the young family's priority. They never owned their own home, living instead in modest apartments in working-class neighborhoods on Chicago's northwest side. Polish, Serbian, and Latvian were among the many languages of Eastern Europe that could be heard on the neighborhood's gritty streets. Railroad tracks and thoroughfares filled with truck, bus, and automobile traffic cut through the area where factories were interlaced with classic Chicago bungalows and apartment buildings, large and small. For much of their growing-up years, the Blagojevich brothers lived on the second floor of a well-kept two-flat. The two boys shared a bedroom in the five-room apartment and were nearly inseparable. Robert has vivid memories of the time his father was about to punish him for playing a prank on his cousins: "He took off his belt . . . but as he started to punish me, Rod stepped in the way and we both got punished for something that I did. And so I'll always be grateful in that case for the loyalty that Rod demonstrated."

Today Robert is one of the few people Rod Blagojevich trusts. It was Robert to whom the governor turned to run Citizens for Blagojevich, his fund-raising operation, after federal investigators bore down on him. When Patrick Fitzgerald moved to freeze the assets in that fund, he indicated he wanted to talk with Robert Blagojevich. Robert let his attorney do all his talking. When the lawyer was asked about Robert, "Would he cooperate and talk to the government?" he replied, "Not a prayer."

Like most young boys, sports dominated the lives of the Blagojevich kids. The gravel parking lot that belonged to the factory just across the street was the arena for hundreds of hours of baseball, basketball, and football. When ice covered the gravel in the winter, hockey sticks came out. Robert was the more gifted athlete, and though Rod was proud of his older brother's skills, he longed to measure up to his brother's performance. His lifelong friend, Michael Ascaridis, the son of Greek immigrants, contends that is part of what makes Rod Blagojevich so competitive today. "A lot of that drive had to do with the fact that his brother and I were a year older," Ascaridis says, "so he was always playing with older kids, and he didn't mature physically as fast as we did. To make up for that, he developed that drive." He remembers Rod insisting that Ascaridis spend hours on the basketball court with him, feeding him the ball so he could perfect his behind-the-back pass. When Rod wanted to make the high school basketball team on which his brother was a star, Robert watched the enormous effort his brother put out. "It was January or December . . . and he was out on the basketball court, shooting, dribbling, doing layups with ice on the court. You've got to give it to a guy who's willing to go out there in those conditions, and he did make the high school team."

As Rade Blagojevich watched his sons becoming typical American kids, he worried that they were losing touch with his own Serbian culture. He wanted the boys raised in a Serbian home, and that meant going to the Serbian Eastern Orthodox church every Sunday. Both Robert and Rod served as altar boys. Sunday mornings could be grueling as the boys were on their feet for two and a half hours carrying religious icons from place to place, moving candles, and following the priest as he delivered the Liturgy in old Slavonic—all tiresome rituals for two boys longing to be on the basketball court.

Lessons in Serbian history and culture were learned in an after-school program. The boys liked their music lessons except that they had to carry their strange looking Serbian instruments, the mandolin-like *tamburica*, on the bus to their lessons. Rod Blagojevich remembered those trips, thinking, "I'm going to get my ass kicked if somebody in the neighborhood sees me with this." But they learned to like playing their *tamburicas* and even traveled with a Serbian orchestra to perform around the city. Rod had a beautiful voice and became an attraction as the orchestra's soloist, singing Serbian folk songs until his voice began to change. He relished the attention his early performances brought him.

For two weeks every summer, Rod and his brother were packed off to Libertyville, Illinois, for a two-week church camp. Serbian kids from around the Midwest came to the camp run by the priests from the St. Sava Serbian Orthodox Monastery. Preserving Serbian culture and strengthening ties in the Serbian community by bringing its children together was the philosophy and foundation of the camp. After the required morning church service, campers would take classes in literature, history, and the Serbian language. The afternoons were more to Rod's liking, with time for baseball, swimming, and trips to the nearby theme park, Great America. Father Ivanovic Aleksander was a counselor when Rod was a camper and remembers him as a cute, outgoing boy, with lots of girl-friends and an older brother who watched over him.

Their father's politics were shaped by World War II and his years as a prisoner of war. He was staunchly pro-American and passionately anti-Communist. Robert Blagojevich remembers that his dad acted almost irratio-nally about communism—like the time he took both small boys to a downtown rally protesting Marshal Tito's visit to Chicago. Their father lost sight of them in the swirling crowds and found them only because they were frantically waving the "Down with Tito" placards he had given them. After the war, Rade Blagojevich never forgave Allied lead-ers Winston Churchill and Franklin Roosevelt for allowing Communists to take power in Yugoslavia. He became a loyal Republican out of gratitude to General Dwight D. Eisenhower, who had liberated his POW camp, and he supported Richard Nixon for his anti-Communist views.

But it was a divided household. Millie Blagojevich had grown up as a Roosevelt Democrat, steeped in the Demo-cratic ward politics of her old Chicago neighborhood. The Blagojeviches' alderman was the most powerful ward boss in the city, Thomas Keane. Richard J. Daley's floor leader, Keane went to jail when Rod was in high school for making millions off illegal secret land deals. (From his prison cell Keane managed to install his wife as alderman.

Her successor trod the well-worn Chicago corruption path, going to jail in 1987 for tax fraud.) Millie supported the first Mayor Daley and was grateful for her job as a ticket taker for the Chicago Transit Authority, the city's transportation system. Both boys remember spirited dinner-table discussions highlighted by their parents' clashing political views. The sons mirrored their parents' conflicting preferences: Robert became a rock-ribbed Republican while Rod began his political career as a Democrat. Rod does admit to voting for Ronald Reagan in 1980 and 1984, and to this day he claims Richard Nixon as a hero.

While Rade Blagojevich was thrilled to be in a country that offered him freedom and opportunity, he had a difficult time finding jobs that paid enough to support his family. He took any job offered, no matter how demeaning. One of the not-so-good jobs was working as an exterminator. The boys remember the smell of the harsh chemicals that would fill the small apartment when their father came home at night. He once tried his hand at becoming an entrepreneur, opening a small neighborhood laundry where he and Millie washed and folded their customers' clothes. But the timing was unfortunate as coin-operated laundromats were just coming into vogue, and the business went under. Rade found his next job at a small steel plant on the city's North Side. On summer nights he would bring the boys to the plant where the hot flames from the blast furnaces lit up the street. "This is how hard I work," his boys recounted in a *Chicago Magazine* story. "You guys can chose to work like this. It's honorable work. You can make a good living. Or you can choose to be good in school and be a gentleman."

Years later, to honor his father and because it was good politics, Rod Blagojevich held several of his major campaign rallies in that same steel plant where his father had once worked. He often filled his campaign speeches with references to the values of hard work, honesty, and a love of freedom, all instilled in him by his immigrant parents. Robert says he and his brother felt the pressure to succeed in order to justify the sacrifices their parents had made. "They always instilled in us the idea that you can be anything you want to be. The United States allows you to do that. We're going to sacrifice and educate you both, and we expect you to do something with it.'"

Schoolwork didn't come as easily to Rod as it did to his older brother. But he did develop an early love for history, particularly the history of American presidents. Millie bought a set of the World Book encyclopedia for the boys on the installment plan. Rod was thrilled and occupied himself by reading the volumes for hours on end. Soon he could name all the presidents in order, a feat he can still perform today. Nurturing his interest, Millie next bought him a set of little statues of the presidents. Not content simply to memorize their names, Rod began badgering his brother and his friends to participate in mock presidential elections. This was not a small operation. He would write up ballots, pitting his favorite presidents against one another in an election for "best president." Next he would distribute the ballots at school, at church, in the neighborhood, and to friends on the street. Then, with his brother's help, he would collect the ballots, tabulate the results, and announce the winner on his very own election night. The big winner was, almost always, Abraham Lincoln. This was Illinois, after all.

Although he wasn't a superior student, Rod's ability to memorize—some even say he has a photographic memory—got him through many of his classes. As a teenager he filled three-by-five index cards with quotes he would memorize and carefully file in old cigar boxes. Sometimes he would memorize entire poems. One of his favorites, Rudyard Kipling's "If," he first heard when it was part of a halftime special during a Chicago Bears football game. He was mesmerized by the sight of the game's best players as they ran down the field to the words of the poem. He looked it up in the library the next day and memorized it at once. He loved the combative nature of the poem, the description of what it took to be a man, and today he often refers to it when asked to describe his political philosophy. At the first press conference after his arrest, reporters were baffled when Blagojevich recited the first stanza of "If." But for the embattled governor the words best described the situation he found himself in.

> *If you can keep your head when all about you*
> *Are losing theirs and blaming it on you,*
> *If you can trust yourself when all men doubt you*
> *But make allowance for their doubting too,*
> *If you can wait and not be tired by waiting,*
> *Or being lied about, don't deal in lies,*
> *Or being hated, don't give way to hating . . .*

He left it there before getting to the lines that say:

> *Hold on when there is nothing in you*
> *Except the Will which says to them: "Hold On!"*

But he had emblazoned those lines in his memory as well.

Rod Blagojevich's mother also gets the credit—or the blame—for another of Rod's lifelong passions, Elvis Presley. In the late sixties, when the Beatles were a sensation and Bob Dylan and Mick Jagger were becoming icons,

Millie and her son were curled up on the couch, watching Elvis movies. Robert says his brother was "fascinated with this charismatic guy who's running around swinging with the girls, singing and being the center of attention. You know, Elvis was good to his mother. Elvis came from humble origins. And he could identify with all of that."

Long after most of America had lost its fascination with Elvis, Rod Blagojevich nurtured the legend. Just as he now peppers his speeches with references to the values of his immigrant parents, he rarely leaves out a lyric from an Elvis tune. After the governor was arrested, he held an impromptu news conference, telling reporters, "Hang loose, to quote Elvis." Meanwhile U.S. Attorney Patrick Fitzgerald was forging ahead with his investigation, perhaps humming "Jailhouse Rock."

When Rod began his freshman year in high school in 1972, young Americans were still loudly protesting the Vietnam War. But in the Blagojevich household, there was no such dissent. Rade Blagojevich would not hear of it. "We were supporters of U.S. policy," says Robert. "We were *not* opposed to the war." That same family characteristic was demonstrated again when Rod Blagojevich became a member of Congress. He was the only Illinois Democrat on October 10, 2002, to vote in favor of authorizing the war in Iraq.

The permissive hippie culture of those turbulent sixties and seventies was never of interest to the Blagojevich boys. Mike Ascaridis recalls that when he and Rod would go to the school playground to shoot hoops, "you'd come up to the park dribbling and you could smell the marijuana smoke. Hippies just hanging around smoking pot and drinking beer—that never appealed to us at all." But the mod fashions of the seventies—now that was something that did appeal to young Rod. Always conscious of his personal appearance, he paid careful attention to his clothes—and lavished care on his luxurious head of hair. Even though money was always tight at home, Rod refused to go to the local barber, instead traveling outside the neighborhood to a hair *stylist*.

Rod didn't join his classmates as they went on to Foreman, his neighborhood high school. Rather, he followed his brother to Lane Tech, a school with a better academic reputation. And though in those days scholarship was not his priority, Lane Tech also had a better basketball team, on which Rod hoped to join his brother. Unable to match his brother's skills, either academically or athletically, he transferred to Foreman in his junior year. A broken wrist in practice that season put an end to his hoop dreams.

In his senior year Rod became interested in boxing, and it was his knowledge of American presidents that led him to the sport. He was fascinated by the fact that Teddy Roosevelt, one of his heroes, had overcome a sickly childhood by taking up boxing. By the time Roosevelt got to Harvard, he was good enough to make the boxing team. Robert had left for college during Rod's senior year, but he remembers sending his brother a Teddy Roosevelt quote, "about the man in the arena whose face was marred by blood and tears and sweat while the meek sit and criticize those in the arena." Inspired, Rod signed up with a boxing coach at the local Chicago Park District fieldhouse. Soon he had worked his way up to the Golden Gloves competition, winning his very first fight, though both he and his opponent landed in the infirmary with black eyes and bruises. The second bout proved less successful for the young Blagojevich. A coach told the *Chicago Tribune* that he lost because he kept his gloves up to defend his face. Even though Rod suffered defeat, he was cocky enough to ask the *Tribune* photographer to take his picture, winking as the shutter snapped.

That short boxing career apparently taught Blagojevich life lessons he still values today. "Now he's in the arena for real and is assured that outside influences don't affect how he thinks about himself, how he thinks about issues, and how committed he is to his political agenda," says brother Robert.

Rade Blagojevich worked away from home for most of his boys' high school years. Determined to find the money to send his two sons to college, he learned of high-paying jobs working on the Alaskan pipeline. A Serbian friend working in Fairbanks arranged to bring Rade to Alaska, where he found a job. For the next several years Rade came home only once every six months. It was a strain on the family, but Rod got to join his father in Alaska during the summers. He wasn't old enough to work on the pipeline. But he spent ten hours a day, seven days a week, washing dishes for the workers—which he says showed him the value of hard work and netted him several thousand dollars for college tuition.

It took some of the pressure off the family resources when Robert won a baseball scholarship to the University of Tampa. With a lackluster grade-point average, brought down by a D in algebra, and only an 18 or 19 on his ACT, Rod was offered no scholarships. But he followed his brother to Tampa the following year. The land of beaches and palm trees was an exotic choice for two boys from Chicago's northwest side. Yet though it was beautiful and warm, it was simply not a good fit for Rod. He was homesick when he mailed a long-shot application to the prestigious Northwestern University—and it paid off. He was accepted and transferred in his junior year. Northwestern wasn't a perfect fit either for the brash city kid from a working-class neighborhood, a kid who loved Elvis Presley while other undergraduates on the Evanston campus were listening to Pink Floyd, Michael Jackson, and the Police. With one of the wealthiest student populations in the country, the school made Rod feel unsure of himself. He couldn't afford to live on campus anyway. He lived at home to save money and got a job delivering pizzas. He majored in history and graduated in 1979 with a B.S. degree, ready to conquer something.

4

Political Stepping-Stones

IN 1980, the summer after he graduated from Northwestern, Rod Blagojevich and his friend Mike Ascaridis decided to treat themselves to New York City. Neither of them had ever been there, and they were excited about experiencing firsthand the sights and sounds of the Big Apple. Blagojevich insisted on one particular stop on their itinerary that was unusual for two twenty-somethings: he was determined to meet one of his father's heroes, Richard Nixon. Six years earlier the former president had been driven from office by the Watergate scandals, which only made him more intriguing to Blagojevich. He had followed the Watergate hearings and yearned to meet the man who had dominated so much of the news of the 1970s. In a magazine Blagojevich learned that Nixon went on regular walks in his Upper East Side neighborhood, even the location and time he left his townhouse. So Blagojevich and Ascaridis staked out the spot and were thrilled when Nixon appeared on schedule. Blagojevich got Nixon's autograph and had a picture taken with him—it shows a grinning Blagojevich in a pair of running shorts standing next to the disgraced former president. Blagojevich could not have known then that almost thirty years later he would share another date with Nixon. On January 9, 2009, the Illinois House of Representatives voted to impeach Governor Rod Blagojevich. It would have been Richard Nixon's ninety-sixth birthday.

Back in Chicago and with his bachelor's degree in his pocket, Blagojevich considered law school. But first he would have to make some money. A friend found him a job in the office of the Cook County Recorder of Deeds, and Rod's father was able to arrange a second job as a Serbo-Croatian interpreter for the Cook County courts. Although the Blagojevich family spoke the language at home, Rod had grown up as an American kid, thinking and speaking English. One story has it that in interpreting the charges against a Bulgarian man accused of criminal sexual assault, Blagojevich used the Bulgarian word for "cannon" instead of "gun." The man vigorously denied he had ever used a cannon—and was not charged with the crime. Blagojevich later admitted to this mistranslation as a travesty of justice.

His job as an interpreter also brought him in contact with one of Chicago's most powerful aldermen, Edward R. Vrdolyak, a Croatian American who ran the southeast side's Tenth Ward. Vrdolyak was one of the few aldermen who dared to challenge the elder Daley. In 1972 Vrdolyak and a group of young turks mounted what was called the "coffee rebellion"—because they plotted their strategy over coffee at a hotel near City Hall. They weren't working for political reform; they just wanted their share of power. But Daley would have none of it and quickly slapped down their rebellion.

Daley's death introduced a changing political landscape. It was still unsettled when Rod Blagojevich was called on to interpret for a Croatian client of Vrdolyak's law practice. An aide to Vrdolyak was impressed with Blagojevich and suggested the alderman meet with him. A time and place was arranged, but one of the young interpreter's former Northwestern professors steered him away from the meeting, cautioning him to avoid Chicago politics at a time he was thinking about getting into law school.

Although Blagojevich aspired to study law at Northwestern, a low score on his LSAT exam sunk him. He scoured the country for a law school with a strong reputation that would nevertheless accept him with his dubious test scores. He set his sights on Pepperdine University in Malibu, California, on the sunny beaches of the Pacific, home of the rich and famous. Blagojevich's friends say he was attracted to the area because Richard Nixon had roots in Malibu.

At Pepperdine, Rod Blagojevich and Alonzo "Lon" Monk became fast friends and running buddies. Although Monk was a Southern California boy who grew up in Redondo Beach, he liked the feisty, street-smart kid from Chicago who shared his love of running. The two became even closer when they both signed up for a semester of study in London and lived in the same hotel. A favorite London memory they shared was watching a Tommy Heard/Sugar Ray Leonard fight live from Las Vegas at 3 a.m. at Piccadilly Circus.

Monk says Blagojevich was a good student but not one to keep his nose in his books. Rod, he recalls, had an unusual approach to school. "He was different in law school from most of my friends in that law school was not going to control his life, you know, he was going to control law school. He did a lot of reading, a lot of running, lifting weights—it was part of his life, but it was not all of his life." His professors saw him much the same way—a bright student who applied himself when he had to but liked to set his own agenda. A pattern emerged that could be traced through his life: a disdain for detail, for the everyday nitty-gritty work that is often necessary to complete a job. Rod loved to read, but he didn't spend a lot of time on his law school reading assignments. Instead he read the history books he had always enjoyed. In 1983 he graduated in the middle of his class and immediately returned to Chicago.

Some of his law school classmates remain his closest friends to this day. Lon Monk was groomsman in Blagojevich's wedding, then gave up a career as a sports agent to become Blagojevich's legal counsel when he became a congressman. The two spent many long hours considering whether Blagojevich should run for governor. When the answer was decided as yes, Monk agreed to manage the campaign. After the victory, he became the governor's chief of staff. When Blagojevich was reelected in 2006, Monk left to become a lobbyist with a fistful of clients who did business with the state. Citing the close relationship between the two men, Patrick Fitzgerald ordered a wiretap on Monk's cell phone in November 2008. That tap helped bring about the governor's arrest.

Rod Blagojevich hoped his Pepperdine law degree would open doors to a major downtown law firm in Chicago, but no offers came his way. He was experiencing the reality of the mantra for doing business in the City of the Big Shoulders—*we don't want nobody nobody sent.* Unless you got your job interview through someone with political connections, you would not get the job. And young Rod Blagojevich simply wasn't connected. Not yet.

He ended up taking a job as a clerk in the office of the man he had declined to meet just two years earlier—Alderman Edward Vrdolyak, who by this time was known as "Fast Eddie" for his ability to hammer out a deal in a hurry. The clerk job came through his father, Rade, who had a friend in Vrdolyak's Tenth Ward. The ward had a large population of Serbs and Croatians, many of whom worked in the steel mills that lined the lakefront on Chicago's southeast side and in nearby Gary, Indiana. The mills had begun to shut down and times were tough, but Vryolak was making a good living representing his constituents both at City Hall and in the courtroom.

Most homes in the Tenth Ward were small bungalows set on standard-size city lots—25 feet across the front and 125 feet deep. For his own home Vrdolyak had managed to put four lots together, persuading the city to close off an alley. On the plot he built a huge house with a basketball court and a swimming pool in the backyard. News stories accused Vrdolyak of corruption. They reported that much of the work on his house was being done by city workers, using city materials. But "Fast Eddie" *was* connected, and he was never charged with an offense.

Rod Blagojevich became a clerk in Vrdolyak's office just at the time Harold Washington was elected the first black mayor of Chicago as the white vote split between Mayor Jane Byrne and challenger Richard M. Daley in the Democratic primary. White aldermen, led by Vrdolyak, then nearly paralyzed the operation of city government by refusing to confirm Washington's appointees and blocking the passage of his reform legislation. The City Council battles were so intense that Chicago in those days came to be called "Beirut on the Lake." Vrdolyak's faction had twenty-nine votes in the Council, one less than was needed to override a veto by Washington. That left the mayor with no choice but to govern by veto. The conflict eventually caused black aldermen and white liberal reformers to go to court to ask that the city's wards be redistricted, claiming that race had been used unfairly in drawing the ward boundaries. The courts agreed and in 1986 ordered special aldermanic elections. That gave Mayor Harold Washington the 25–25 split he needed to finally pass his legislation. As the presiding officer of the City Council, the mayor could cast the tie-breaking vote. Although the battles between the "Vrdolyak 29" and the "Washington 21" were characterized as all about race, in fact they had more to do with power. Who would control the machinery of the Democratic party in Chicago? Who would pass out the contracts and reap the benefits that came as part of running the city?

There was always an aura of corruption surrounding "Fast Eddie" Vrdolyak because of his slick political and business dealings. An attempted murder charge was filed against him in 1960. It was eventually dropped, but it gave him a reputation for toughness that he actually relished. He was censured twice by the Illinois Bar Association, and in 2005 his law license was suspended for thirty days for double-billing clients he represented in sexual harassment cases.

But the feds never moved against Vrdolyak until Patrick Fitzgerald came to town. How ironic it was that he was eventually brought down as part of Fitzgerald's wide-ranging investigation of the governor—whom "Fast Eddie" had given his first real job as a law clerk. Vrdolyak often said he talked to everyone as though they were wearing a wire—even his wife. He pleaded guilty on November 3, 2008, to four counts of federal fraud and bribery charges, trapped by a friend wearing a wire. In true "Fast Eddie" style, however, Vrdolyak became one of the few who got the best of Fitzgerald's prosecutor when a federal judge sentenced him to five years' probation for his crimes. The judge chastised the prosecutors, calling them "greedy" for asking for a forty-one-month sentence for Vrdolyak. "God is great," a smiling Vrdolyak proclaimed as he left the courtroom.

In 1983 Blagojevich spent almost as much time shooting hoops on Vrdolyak's backyard basketball court as he did clerking in his law office. Life was good. But all that changed when he failed the bar exam on his first try. Studying seriously for the next exam, he left Vrdolyak's office and spent his time cramming with his law books. He passed the bar in 1984 but still couldn't seem to land a spot in a big-time law firm. He took another clerking job at the Attorney's Title Guaranty Fund. He managed to get a little legal business on the side and was finally able to set up shop for himself when he rented a room in the offices of Sheldon Sorosky, a criminal defense lawyer. Blagojevich was grateful to Sorosky and kept in touch with him through the years. When Governor Blagojevich found himself under arrest by the FBI and facing federal charges, Sheldon Sorosky was the lawyer he called.

The future governor's next job again came the "Chicago way." A friend knew a friend who knew of a position with Richard M. Daley's Cook County state's attorney's office.

The younger Daley ran the office well, and everyone knew he had ambitions to follow in his father's footsteps as mayor of Chicago. The state's attorney was a high-profile figure, good for someone who might want to go into big-time politics some day, and Richie Daley was willing to wait it out. The friend got Blagojevich the job in Daley's office, where he was assigned to traffic court—considered the "dumping ground" for novice attorneys. But Blagojevich impressed the people he worked with. A traffic court prosecutor at the time observed, "You knew he was going places. He was a mover and a shaker, never stood still." One afternoon Blagojevich confided to another prosecutor that someday he would like to run for president.

After his traffic court service, the young prosecutor was sent to the courts at Fifty-first and Wentworth, in the tough Area One Police District that borders the Dan Ryan Expressway. The courts sat at the south end of the massive housing projects that lined State Street, the Robert Taylor Homes. Blagojevich worked out of a small, bare office, which he shared with several other assistant state's attorneys, next to the formal courtroom where their cases were heard. The cases reflected the woes of the neighborhood: harrowing stories about lives damaged by drugs, guns, and domestic violence. Crack cocaine hit Chicago's streets heavily in the 1980s, and a huge number of cases involved that growing subculture. Those who worked with Blagojevich at the time say he was bright and obviously ambitious, but they questioned his work ethic. He did his work but rarely showed up at the Fifty-first Street offices, swooping in just at the last minute to take a client to court.

While at Area One, Blagojevich befriended a young African American who shined shoes in the lobby. Paris

Thompson was thirteen years old when Blagojevich first sat down on a police station bench to have his shoes shined. He struck up a conversation with the young teenager, telling him he too had shined shoes as a kid. It was true. When Millie Blagojevich took a job in the factory across the street from their home, she set both boys up with shoe shining jobs after school in the factory's reception area. That way she knew where they were, and they could make a little money too.

At first Thompson, who lived in the Robert Taylor Homes, didn't know what to make of Blagojevich. "Here's this white guy—gonna tell me he shined shoes. I mean, I thought this guy really . . . was born with a silver spoon in his mouth. I thought, 'Yeah, this is a bunch of crap.' But after getting to know him, I learned that he came up the hard way. I mean, he *did* shine shoes. He *did* deliver pizza. All I can say is, I just really had a great appreciation for a person like that—and had a great deal of respect for his level of sincerity and commitment to the little people. I considered myself the person locked out. I mean, as a child growing up I was isolated here in public housing, cut off from the rest of the world."

Blagojevich introduced Thompson to a much wider world, taking him along downtown and to the North Side—places Thompson had never seen, though he had grown up in Chicago. He took him to his first baseball game—the Cubs, since Blagojevich was a North Side guy. And he was able to arrange for Thompson to meet some of the ballplayers. Blagojevich also stuck up for Thompson when another shoe shine kid stole a policeman's gun at the station. The police wanted all five of the shoe shine boys kicked out, but Blagojevich knew how much their

$25 a day meant to kids who came from public housing. He intervened, and the kids kept their jobs. Without Blagojevich's help, says Thompson, he probably would have turned to selling drugs like most of his friends.

Even though he was just a kid, Thompson saw that in some ways Blagojevich was more comfortable in the company of a teenager than he was with his fellow state's attorneys. Thompson says the young Serbian from a working-class neighborhood was not like the rest of them. "They didn't like him. I would shine their shoes and they would always try to crack jokes on him. 'Did you buy his suits?' they would ask. He had these cheap suits on. He never hung out with any of those guys. I think part of the problem was he wasn't their kind of people. He didn't come from where they had come from."

Blagojevich kept in touch with Paris Thompson after he left the state's attorney's office. He continued to introduce the South Side kid to a broader world. One thing Thompson says he never understood about Blagojevich is something that puzzles many who know him—his love for Elvis. "Well, you know, he was real weird. I mean, my family always had bad things to say about Elvis Presley. There was never anything good that was said in my community about Elvis. It was always rumored that Elvis said the only thing that a black man can do is shine his shoes and buy his music. But he was a bit of an Elvis fanatic when I met him, and I couldn't understand that. A Serbian—I mean a Serbian guy is not *really* a white guy, I guess. You know, he really *loved* Elvis. He drove this little Alfa Romeo, this little two-seater car, and he would always get in with this Elvis Presley thing. I mean, you know, he'd have all these brushes, brushing his hair and playing these Elvis tapes."

When Paris Thompson grew up he became a high-profile community activist and a well-known Baptist minister on Chicago's South Side, and changed his name. Reverend Bamani Obadele helped get out the black vote in Blagojevich's first gubernatorial campaign. The governor then appointed him to a $65,000-a-year job overseeing adoption and foster programs for the Illinois Department of Children and Family Services. But within two years Reverend Obadele resigned amid charges that $62,754 in payments from DCFS contractors had made their way into the reverend's personal account rather than going to the state.

In December 2008 WLS-TV in Chicago broke a story that Blagojevich had more going on in the mid-1980s than his assistant state's attorney job. A well-known FBI informant who was a key witness in federal cases resulting in dozens of convictions in the 1980s and 1990s told investigative reporter Chuck Goudie that Blagojevich had been a small-time bookmaker on the North Side and regularly paid a street tax to the mob. The informant, Robert Cooley, had once been a mob-connected criminal defense lawyer who had begun cooperating with the FBI in 1986. The terms of Cooley's cooperation required him to report any illegal activity he had seen. One item he passed on to prosecutors was that a young state's attorney, Rod Blagojevich, was running a small sports bookie ring and paying protection to the mob. Cooley says he knew that because at the time he was running a small bookie operation himself, and paying a street tax to the same people. (Bookies pay street taxes to the organized crime syndicate in exchange for being able to operate. Failure to pay can mean a visit to the trunk of a car or the bottom of Lake

Michigan.) According to the TV report, Cooley told the FBI that Blagojevich "regularly paid a street tax to Robert 'Bobby the boxer' Abbinanti, a convicted outfit gambling collector." At the time Cooley gave this information to the FBI, prosecutors had no interest in the small-time bookie operation of an unknown state's attorney. When Blagojevich first ran for governor, Cooley went back to the FBI hoping they would pick up the gambling case, but he was told that the statute of limitations had long passed. When asked about the charges, the governor denied having ever run a bookie operation and denied knowing Robert Cooley. Abbinanti, now a legitimate business-man after six years in a federal penitentiary on gambling charges, says he never knew Blagojevich and never collected street taxes from him.

So, was Rod Blagojevich a small-time bookie in 1985? Chuck Goudie of WLS-TV says, "Well, this is one of those situations where I wasn't there. I'm depending on somebody that the feds depended on, a federal witness named Cooley, whom they put their trust in with federal cases that resulted in lots of people going to jail. If I wasn't comfortable with what Cooley said being true, I wouldn't have put it on the air."

No matter what else Blagojevich was doing besides his job as an assistant state's attorney, he was growing tired of driving to the South Side and unhappy with his low salary. He wanted more, and in 1987 he left the state's attorney's staff to take a job with the firm where he had once rented office space, Sorosky and Kaplan. He handled mostly workmen's compensation cases, but he soon lost interest in the tedious work and within five months set out to start a practice of his own.

Blagojevich found a small space on the North Side where he set up a neighborhood law office. He hired his mother as his receptionist. The arrangement didn't always work out: she often nagged her son about showing up late for appointments—a lifelong problem. Once, when Blagojevich was trying to sign up a new client, his mother stormed into the office. "She throws this telephone message at me: 'Gladys Shiba just called, and she's disgusted with the way you're handling her case,' and storms out. And this potential client is looking at all this."

While working at his new practice in 1988, Rod Blagojevich experienced two events that completely changed his life. His father died from a massive stroke, and he met his future wife, Patricia Mell.

5

Get Me a Candidate

AT AGE SEVENTY-SEVEN, life was good for Rade Blagojevich. A vigorous and proud man, he still worked around the house and was finally able to enjoy life at his own pace. His sons had graduated from college, and at last he and Millie were able to kick back a bit. But that was before a massive stroke took him to his knees. Rade found himself unable to walk or speak. He had been visiting his son Robert in Nashville when the stroke felled him. He was rushed to the emergency room where doctors worked frantically to reverse the damage to his body. But it was not to be. He was flown back to Chicago but was never able to return to his home again. He died ten months later. Rod Blagojevich was devastated by the loss of his father. For the first time he began thinking seriously about his own life and his own mortality. Perhaps it was time for a thirty-one-year-old bachelor to settle down, to find someone to share his life and begin a family of his own.

In another North Side neighborhood an attractive, dark-haired young woman was having similar thoughts. Twenty-three-year-old Patti Mell, a recent graduate of the University of Illinois with a degree in economics, had just broken up with her boyfriend. Her father, Richard Mell, the powerful alderman of the Thirty-third Ward, was beginning to worry about his daughter as she moped around the house after the breakup. He suggested she come with him to a ward fund-raiser he was holding that night in a North Side German restaurant. It would be good for her just to get out of the house, he told her.

A friend had persuaded Rod Blagojevich to come to the same fund-raiser. Patti knew who he was. She had met the judge who presided over the courtrooms at Fifty-first and Wentworth, where Rod had worked as an assistant state's attorney. That meeting occurred at a summer wedding, when Patti was seated next to him during the reception. The judge—maybe with a fix-up in mind—told her about a dynamic young state's attorney who worked in his courtroom. And so, at the fund-raiser, with Patti on his arm, the judge wasted no time in introducing the two unattached and seemingly lonely young people. Certainly Rod Blagojevich wasted no time in capturing the attention of the alderman's attractive daughter. The judge chuckled to himself as he overheard Rod telling her, "If you go out with me, I'm going to show you the time of your life." Later that evening Patti repeated those same words to her father: "Dad, if I go out with him, I'll probably have the time of my life." She accepted Rod's offer.

Mell was delighted to see his daughter happy, and he was impressed with the seemingly charming and outgoing young Blagojevich. Family was important to Mell; he had always been a supportive and protective father for his three children. He did not want them to experience the kind of devastating loss he had felt when his own mother abandoned him when he was five years old. His father and grandparents raised him in Muskegon, Michigan, after his mother took off for New York. She would return every few years or so, "when she needed a few bucks," says Mell, but she never stayed. He credits his grandmother with providing stability in his life but says his upbringing "probably made me the way I am, the fact that I always try to please everybody."

After college in Michigan, Mell headed for Chicago where he met the woman who was to be "the love of my life," Marge Bruzzo. Patti was the first born, and she and her father were always close. Although in later years Patti would be described as cold and standoffish, Mell never saw his daughter that way. He continued to defend her even after the break came over Blagojevich, just as he defended his younger daughter Deborah when she declared she was gay. But all that unhappiness was far in the future the night Rod and Patti went out on their first official date.

Rod took Patti to Shaw's Crab House, an upscale seafood restaurant near the Loop. She told friends afterward, "I met someone who was actually kind of different, interesting. I love to read. I'm a big reader and Rod's a big reader, too . . . so immediately we started talking about what we were reading. We discovered that we had the same tastes in movies and those kinds of things. It was kind of interesting, and I told my friends I had met somebody really cute." Only five months later Patti Mell became even more convinced that Rod might be *the one*. They had been dating often enough to be regarded as a couple. Coming home from a Fourth of July celebration at Patti's great-grandmother's house in Wonder Lake, Wisconsin, Patti remembers, "Rod's radio in his car was broken, and on the way home he sang Elvis to me . . . all the way home—and that's when I kind of knew that he was different and special." Patti told her friends that it took her a while to figure out just what was behind her new boyfriend's fascination—perhaps even an obsession—with Elvis Presley. "I think Elvis just kind of embodies the whole American dream. Elvis comes from nothing. He was the son of a sharecropper—just that wonderful rise to fame. We used to have arguments when we were dating about who was greater—the Beatles or Elvis. And he would always sort of trump me by saying, 'Well, how many Beatles impersonators are around now?'"

Two years later Rod was ready to get married, and Patti accepted his proposal. She says Rod and her father have different interpretations of what actually happened after he asked her to marry him. "My dad says that Rod . . . *asked his permission* to marry me . . . and Rod's version is he wanted to meet with my father to *inform* him that he was going to ask me to marry him. I still don't know which one of those stories is right." It might have been the first hint that Blagojevich and Mell would forever struggle over which one of them was in charge.

The couple chose a date that fell during the Serbian Lenten season, and the Serbian Orthodox priest told them he could not marry them on that day. Patti had been raised Roman Catholic but had drifted away from her church; she did not feel strongly about being married in the Catholic church. And while Rod would have liked to be married in the Serbian Orthodox church, it wasn't as important to him as it would have been if his father had

still been alive. Finally the couple settled on the Alice Mil-
lar Chapel at Rod's alma mater, Northwestern University,
with a Protestant tradition. In the warm glow of light from
its glorious stained-glass window, and with beautiful music
filling every corner of the church, a Presbyterian minister
conducted the ceremony as Dick Mell gave his daughter
away. On Rod and Patti's wedding day, it seemed as
though they would surely live happily ever after.

Dick Mell had secured his prospective son-in-law a
job on the city payroll just six months after Blagojevich
began dating Patti. That was what Mell did. He found jobs
for people who supported him and his Thirty-third Ward
organization. He was a successful businessman, founding
an automobile parts manufacturing firm with his wife in
the early 1970s. The business provided a good living for
Mell and his three children and enabled him to indulge in
his passion—politics.

Richard J. Daley was mayor when the brash young
Mell first stuck his toe into the political waters as a candidate. In 1972 he ran as an Independent against Daley's ward
committeeman in the Thirty-third Ward, where Mell lived.
Daley's candidate trounced him by five hundred votes. But
Daley's wrath didn't end there. He was still on the warpath
in the wake of the battles at the 1968 Democratic National
Convention in Chicago. The challenges to the old-line
party structure that became apparent at that event were still
reverberating among Democrats and in the nation.

Dick Mell had watched the protests of 1968 from the
sidelines, but four years later he wanted to get involved.
Not only did he run against Daley's candidate for ward
committeeman, he was part of the Illinois delegation that
engineered the removal of Mayor Daley and his delegates

from the 1972 Democratic National Convention in Miami for violating Democratic party rules. It was a time of enormous change in the Democratic party—-and ultimately the time of Richard Nixon.

Three years later in Chicago, in 1975, Mell won his race for alderman in the Thirty-third Ward. The next year he won the powerful Democratic party post as ward committeeman, in charge of handing out patronage jobs. Within a decade he had achieved the positions he needed in order to build a powerful ward organization. Although Mell initially ran against Daley's organization, he decided he would not get far as an independent political reformer. He would have to be an *organization* politician. But he didn't wish to depend on Mayor Daley for success, so Mell built his own organization within Daley's empire. He did it the old-fashioned Chicago way, by taking care of the people who worked the precincts for him. By the mid-1980s the *Chicago Tribune* was reporting that Mell's Thirty-third Ward Democratic organization could put together close to a thousand foot soldiers to work the precincts. And almost half of them had city jobs. By using patronage skillfully, Dick Mell had built his own power base.

Mell's most visible moment in city politics came in 1987 after the death of Chicago's first black mayor, Harold Washington. Because the City Council would have to vote to fill the vacancy, all hell was breaking loose in the city's political arena. In a rowdy late-night Council session, as factions fought to seat their own candidate, Mell famously stood on top of his desk in the Council chambers, shouting at the top of his lungs and demanding to be recognized as the divided body wrestled with the biggest question in Chicago politics: who would succeed Harold Washington?

Mell had sided with Vrdolyak and had worked against Mayor Washington at every turn. At that raucus City Council meeting Mell helped orchestrate a political move that returned the anti-Washington forces to power.

Rod Blagojevich slid easily into Mell's organization. City payroll records show he was being paid by as many as four different City Council committees in one year. But Blagojevich told the *Chicago Tribune* he never worked in City Hall; rather, he said, he worked in Mell's ward service office where he organized community events and held free legal clinics. The U.S. attorney's office launched an investigation into ghost payrolling at that time, concentrating on whether some of those listed on city payrolls, like Blagojevich, were being paid for doing no work. A handful of Mell's office workers were questioned, but the investigation never resulted in indictments. Blagojevich was snagged by the city's ethics ordinance, however, when he represented legal clients from his private law practice in personal injury and workmen's compensation cases. The ethics ordinance bars city employees from representing personal clients in cases against the city. The ethics complaint against Blagojevich went to the City Council Rules Committee, chaired by—who else?—Alderman Dick Mell. The charges were dropped.

Rod and Patti Blagojevich had been married for two years when the phone rang one Sunday evening. Dick Mell, on the other end of the line, needed a candidate to run for state representative—and he needed one *now*. "Are you interested?" he asked Rod. It was the beginning of Rod Blagojevich's political career.

The seat in the Illinois House of Representatives had opened up when legislative districts were redrawn in 1991.

Mell thought he had lined up a candidate his organization would support, but that individual had defected at the last minute. In Chicago an election for a state representative is not usually in the forefront of voters' minds. A city aldermanic seat is much more important, and so a politician with a strong precinct organization—someone like Dick Mell—can have a major impact in electing a state candidate, especially if the candidate isn't a strong one.

But Rod Blagojevich turned out to be a strong candidate. He was personable, outgoing, and seemed to like retail campaigning—hitting the streets and pressing the flesh. He stood at windy bus stops on freezing Chicago mornings, shook hands at neighborhood grocery stores, and walked the ward's precincts door-to-door. Patti Blagojevich has good memories of that first race: "It was funny because, even though I'm from a political family, when my father first got elected I was only ten years old—so I never got involved, and I was *really* involved in Rod's first race. I knocked on doors four nights a week, and that was a cold, cold winter—but it was a lot of fun. In some respects that first election was the most fun because you're the most idealistic and you've never done it before and everything's fresh and new."

Two other Democratic powerhouses, Congressman Dan Rostenkowski and Forty-seventh Ward committeeman Ed Kelly, backed different candidates in the race. Mell told Blagojevich, the first-time candidate, that winning would not be easy. "I was pessimistic, I'm always pessimistic, and he was upbeat about it, and I kept thinking, 'this kid doesn't know what he's doing out there.' How can things look that good when he's in Rostenkowski's ward and Kelly's ward and those guys should be able to annihilate him because state rep races are sort of a *controlled* election. But he was a great candidate."

Dick Mell poured his heart and soul—and his formidable organization—into the race. Those close to Mell said he came to look upon Blagojevich more like a son than a son-in-law. Mell's own son, Richard Mell, Jr., wasn't much interested in becoming a candidate and didn't have Blagojevich's outgoing personality or charisma. His dad, true to tradition, had found Rich Mell a job on the city payroll, working at O'Hare International Airport. At the time, neither of the two Mell daughters, Patti and Deborah, wanted to follow their father's footsteps into politics either, though sixteen years later Mell would help engineer the election of Deborah to a seat in the Illinois General Assembly.

On election night Mell went to bed early, convinced Blagojevich would lose. His wife woke him to tell him that Blagojevich was winning precincts in Dan Rostenkowski's ward. Rod Blagojevich, the political neophyte, had won the vote in the powerful Rostenkowski's own neighborhood. "That's it," shouted Mell, "Rod's won!"

Blagojevich went to Springfield for his first term as very much the creation of Dick Mell and the Thirty-third Ward Democratic political organization. From the start it bugged him that he was seen only as Dick Mell's son-in-law. He always made a great effort to say that Mell *never* influenced his votes. His fellow state representative and Springfield roommate Jay Hoffman, from downstate Illinois, agreed: "I know for a fact that he doesn't call Dick Mell and say, 'How should I vote on this?' As a matter of fact, if Dick Mell *were* to weigh in on an issue, it may offend him and he might vote the other way."

Blagojevich concentrated on issues that made use of his legal and criminal defense background. From the beginning he spoke out on hot-button issues that made him stand out in the crowd of other legislators. He sponsored the first truth-in-sentencing legislation in Illinois, which required criminals to serve at least 85 percent of their prison term before becoming eligible for parole. He also introduced a bill to take guns away from people with domestic battery convictions. Jay Hoffman says Blagojevich took some tough political stands in those days—such as voting for property tax caps, which were not supported by Democratic party leaders or the unions. He also took some progressive positions that were not necessarily attuned to the more conservative nature of the blue-collar voters in his district. He strongly supported pro-choice for women and gay rights. Still, he was regarded as somewhat of a lightweight by his Illinois House colleagues. Even then it was clear that Blagojevich wasn't much interested in the legislative process. He rarely showed up for committee meetings, and his fellow Democrats often had to go out and round him up for important votes.

Barbara Flynn Currie was serving as a state legislator from Chicago's Hyde Park neighborhood when Blagojevich won his seat. She summed up the way he was widely viewed in those early days of his political career: "He's a bright guy, a charming guy—a good raconteur. He was understood to be somebody who got there because somebody sent him—namely, Dick Mell. And I don't think he was perceived as being just a hack. But he was definitely seen as a lightweight. Smart—but a lightweight." Currie's first impression had not changed when, sixteen years later, she chaired the Illinois House Impeachment Committee against Governor Blagojevich.

While in Springfield during his legislative years, Blagojevich loved the political life. But he also kept up with two of his other passions—running and Elvis Presley. His roommate, Jay Hoffman, was not enamored of either. It was not just that Blagojevich would hit the CD player with blaring Elvis tunes whenever he entered the apartment. It was that he would play the same song over and over again. Sometimes he would drag an unwilling Hoffman along as a running partner.

By the time he was in the legislature, Blagojevich had already run his first marathon. He was a serious runner and spent many early-morning and late-evening hours training to run a successful marathon in under three hours. He liked the way running also helped him clear the cobwebs from his head after battles over what he often considered legislative trivia. He used the endorphins produced by his long runs to keep himself pumped up. His running became a lifelong routine, and though national reporters were surprised when the embattled governor actually went for a run on the day the Illinois legislature was voting on his impeachment, those who knew him well were not surprised at all.

The state representative and his father-in-law soon began to look around for a way that Blagojevich might move up in the political food chain. It was 1994, just at the moment Chicago's almighty congressman Dan Rostenkowski ran into trouble. Although the powerful chairman of the House Ways and Means Committee faced a seventeen-count federal indictment for misusing the powers of his office, he refused to step down and instead mounted a campaign to save his congressional seat. Republicans put up a politically unknown candidate, Michael Flanagan. But with all the fallout against the once-powerful incumbent, Flanagan took the Fifth District congressional seat away from Rostenkowski. While Flanagan and the Republicans were flush with their upset victory, it was no secret that Flanagan was a weak legislator—still practically unknown—from a solidly Democratic district. Everyone who knew anything about Chicago politics recognized that Flanagan would be easy to knock off in the next election.

Initially, though, Mell was nervous about Blagojevich giving up his safe seat as a state representative. He advised his son-in-law that the powerful Thirty-third Ward organization wouldn't have as much impact in a congressional race. "This is like ten state rep races," Mell told him. "My input is going to be a lot less than I had in the state rep race." But Blagojevich was eager. It was unfortunate for the little family that Patti Blagojevich was not on board. She told Rod she had absolutely no intention of moving to Washington, D.C., with their infant daughter, Amy. But by that time Rod was already running.

In the primary election for the congressional seat, Blagojevich squared off against fellow state legislator Nancy Kaszak and Ray Romero, an executive from the Ameritech phone company. Blagojevich and Mell knew the race would not be a pushover, so Mell reached deep into his financial resources for professional help. They hired the highly skilled political media consultant David Axelrod. Years later Axelrod would become the architect of Barack Obama's presidential campaign and then join President Obama in the White House as his chief adviser. But when Blagojevich and Mell came to him, Axelrod's clients were mostly Chicago-area politicians or would-be officeholders, including Richard M. Daley, who was in his second term as mayor. Mell assumed the role of field general, running the precinct operation and bringing in the troops to cover the entire congressional district. Blagojevich squeaked through the primary with 50 percent of the vote and kept right on running into the general election.

He again proved to be a vibrant campaigner traveling his diverse district, which included much more than the blue-collar bungalows that made up the majority of his state legislative district. The Fifth Congressional District stretches from the wealthy and "liberal" North Side neighborhoods along the Chicago lakefront to the northwest side neighborhoods and suburbs around O'Hare airport, home of the "Reagan Democrats" in Chicago— longtime Democrats who had switched to Ronald Reagan in the 1980s.

Whatever race he found himself in, Blagojevich had to deal with his long, befuddling name. That's "Bla-goya-vich," he told voters over and over as he shook hands across the district. The campaign was a strange tangle of positions. Blagojevich, a Democrat, was running as a "reformer" after Rostenkowski went down for corruption. He put his name on the small sponges he handed out to "clean up" the district. Axelrod didn't think much of the sponges, but Blagojevich insisted that voters loved them. His opponent, Michael Flanagan, ran as the Republican who could bring federal dollars back to the district, as Rostenkowski had once done so successfully. In his one term, Flanagan had managed to bring home an $11.3 million grant to address Lake Michigan's receding lakefront. He even persuaded the speaker of the House, Newt

Gingrich, to get personally involved. Gingrich told the *Chicago Tribune* that Flanagan had convinced him "This is not just Chicago's lakefront. This is America's lakefront." But Newt's pitch didn't strike a chord with voters in the district. They were quite simply Democrats.

Blagojevich had not won the support of women's groups when he ran against Nancy Kaszak in the hotly contested primary. But once he earned the nomination, the National Organization for Women gave him a strong endorsement. At a NOW-sponsored rally, Blagojevich told the crowd, "My baby daughter was born two weeks ago. I hope she joins NOW. I hope she joins Planned Parenthood. My opponent is not pro-life, he's *anti-choice*." That brought the NOW members on board. Blagojevich also went after Flanagan for his opposition to gun control: "My opponent has not only voted for the repeal of the ban on assault weapons, he's taken substantial funding from the NRA." In Chicago, where crimes with guns were a big issue, that brought the majority of voters on board.

The congressional battle was the first race in which Rod Blagojevich raised serious money for his campaign. He pulled in more than a million dollars, exceeding the fund-raising of any other Democratic house challenger at the time. In the primary election Nancy Kaszak had run television commercials accusing Blagojevich and Mell of shaking down city contractors and city workers for campaign contributions. When her allegations gained no purchase, Kaszak was criticized for negative campaigning. In the general election Blagojevich outspent Flanagan more than two-to-one. It was an early lesson for the young politician about the value of a well-financed campaign. On election night 1996 Blagojevich coasted to an easy victory with 64 percent of the vote. At Christmastime, just after the election, Dick Mell was in a great mood. He jokingly offered his analysis of the race by showing a reporter his Christmas list—with a question mark next to Rod's name. Mell cracked, "Don't you think I've already bought him enough this year?"

In January 1997 Rod Blagojevich headed to Washington, D.C., without his wife and daughter, ready to make a name for himself in the 105th Congress. He soon found himself bogged down in the daily trivia of the House of Representatives. From his school days, Blagojevich had never enjoyed working on the details. He preferred to put together—and get credit for—the bigger picture. Just four months after he was sworn in, he complained, "There's such an emphasis on rank and seniority. It's contrary to the Jeffersonian notion of meritocracy. In the Illinois General Assembly, one can be recognized out of order. Here it's different." Not only was Blagojevich low man on the seniority totem pole, Democrats were now in the minority in the Congress, making it even more difficult for him to separate himself from the pack of 435 representatives. In the first few months of his term he had been able to cast a vote on only two matters: the creation of a commission to study the economy of American Samoa, and—to him equally boring—a resolution to support an Alabama judge who refused to remove the Ten Commandments from his courtroom. In a town hall meeting back in Chicago, he pointed out that he hadn't received a single question about American Samoa. The frustrated congressman admitted, "There's been very little of substantive impact on people's lives. It is surprising that we're involved in such nonmonumental issues. You think of Henry Clay and the giants in Congress over the last few centuries—or the Missouri Compromise of 1820. And you, well . . ."

Privately, several of Blagojevich's fellow legislators say he never passed much legislation because he was not interested in putting in the necessary time to see a bill through to enactment. A website that tracks congressional votes found that in his four years in Congress, Blagojevich sponsored thirty-seven bills—but thirty-five of them never made it out of committee, and only one was successfully enacted. That bill underscored his efforts for strong gun-control legislation that had begun back in Springfield. The measure allocated $1.25 million to trace guns found at crime sites and for the first time added Chicago to the list of cities that would benefit. As a result, Chicago police were able to trace ten thousand guns in one year, all but ninety-eight of them sold in illegal black-market deals. Blagojevich's gun-control efforts were popular in his congressional district, but he would later learn when he campaigned for governor that gun-control legislation wasn't as popular in rural downstate Illinois.

Congressman Blagojevich did win press attention when he mounted a successful campaign to prevent the navy from shipping Vietnam-era napalm by rail through the Chicago area to an East Chicago, Indiana, disposal plant. At his request the navy agreed to public meetings in the Chicago area to explain the project. After Blagojevich and others aired their concerns, the East Chicago plant that was scheduled to dispose of the napalm canceled its contract, and the navy scrapped its plan. The napalm controversy was the kind of high-profile issue that Blagojevich liked to pursue. He was criticized for inflating the danger of the napalm concern in order to magnify his success in solving the problem. In great sound bites for the evening news, Blagojevich had said publicly that Hiroshima-level explosions were a possibility as the railroad cars carrying the napalm rolled through the dense urban areas of Chicago and northwest Indiana.

Blagojevich suffered a personal blow just after he began his second term in Congress when he lost his mother to lung cancer. He had been unable to be with her to help her through her chemotherapy appointments because of his duties in Washington. That gnawed at him, and though he came home most weekends, it also bothered him that he was missing his daughter Amy's first steps and first words. He had a two-bedroom condo in Washington on Dupont Circle, but Patti rarely came to visit, and the young congressman rattled around in the apartment by himself. He spent many of his hours alone taking long training runs on a hilly Washington golf course. He told friends that the life of a backbencher in Congress didn't seem worth the sacrifices his family was making.

In his second term, an opportunity arose for Blagojevich to become a player on the national stage. In April 1999 NATO forces began a heavy bombing campaign against Serbia in an effort to halt Slobodan Milosevic's brutal campaign of ethnic cleansing in Kosovo. On the ground, three American soldiers were captured and were being held as prisoners of war in Serbia. While the United States followed protocol in trying to free the three captives, the Reverend Jesse Jackson announced he would initiate a humanitarian mission to negotiate their release. President Bill Clinton's State Department was opposed to Jackson's involvement and offered no assistance.

Immediately after the soldiers were captured, Congressman Blagojevich approached the Clinton administration. He cited his Yugoslav family ties and his ability to speak the language, and offered to help in gaining the soldiers' freedom. But he too got a cold shoulder from national security adviser Sandy Berger and White House chief of staff John Podesta.

After Blagojevich read news of Jesse Jackson's mission, he told Jesse Jackson, Jr., the reverend's son, and a congressional colleague, that he had strong contacts in the Serbian-American community who might be able to help. Jackson Sr., realizing the value of Blagojevich's fluency in the Serbian language, knew his contacts could make a difference. He brought Blagojevich into the planning process for the mission.

Reverend Jackson had put together an ecumenical group of religious leaders to make the trip. But he was having trouble persuading Serbian strongman Milosevic to see them, much less allow them near the imprisoned American soldiers. Through his Chicago Serbian contacts, Blagojevich was able to put Jackson in touch with Vuk Draskovic, then the deputy prime minister of Yugoslavia and a Milosevic rival. Jackson, being the media-savvy person he is, hired a documentary film crew to record the efforts of his delegation. In the film Blagojevich is heard speaking in Serbian to Draskovic. He hands the phone off to Jackson who listens to Draskovic say, "I will approach Milosevic tomorrow to explain to allow you in Serbia to see these three soldiers—and even to take them. If you are not in a position to take these soldiers, we will not wait longer than a few days." That conversation convinced the ecumenical group to head to Belgrade the next day. But that evening on television, the story broke that the maverick Draskovic—Blagojevich's contact—had been bounced from his position. Blagojevich remembers Reverend Jackson's words after hearing the news: "Blagojevich, our boy just got fired. You got any others out there?"

As it happened, Blagojevich did. Working his Serbian contacts in Chicago and Belgrade, Blagojevich managed to find enough high-level Serbs to agree to negotiate with Jackson, and the trip was on again. The delegation flew into Zagreb, Croatia, because the Belgrade airport had been closed by NATO bombing. Arriving in Belgrade at long last was an emotional moment for Blagojevich. He was deeply affected by the knowledge that his father had left Yugoslavia in 1941 when Nazi bombs were falling, and here he was arriving in the country for the first time— when NATO bombs were falling.

The group began their first round of negotiations shortly after their bus pulled into Belgrade. The American religious delegation, including Blagojevich, was seated on one side of a long table in a formal dining room in an upscale Belgrade hotel. The Milosevic contingent faced them from the other side of the table as bombs continued to rain down on the city. Blagojevich's fluency in the language became the bridge between the two sides. The first order of business of Jackson's delegation was the release of the soldiers, the reverend emphasizing to the Serbs the goodwill the release would create. But the Milosevic forces wanted more than goodwill. They wanted a guarantee that the NATO bombing would end if the soldiers were released. The American delegation was in no position to make such a promise.

Back home in Chicago, Patti Blagojevich nervously waited to hear from her husband. When she finally got through by telephone to the Belgrade Hyatt Hotel, an English-speaking hotel operator connected her with Rod. She recalled, "He was very kind to me because I knew they were bombing Belgrade every night—and so I asked him, 'Do you see bombs?' It was nighttime. 'Do you see bombs falling?' And he kind of told me a little white lie—and told me, 'No.' But they were bombing all over the place."

Patti Blagojevich was quite right. Congressman Blagojevich remembers looking out his hotel room window and seeing white flashes light up the sky. Just before dawn he decided to deal with the stress of bombing in the way he always dealt with stress, by taking a run. He had brought his friend and chief of staff, John Wyma, to Serbia, so he called John to join him on the streets of Belgrade. The documentary cameras followed them as Rod narrated. "We are going out for an early-morning jog in Belgrade— bombed-out Belgrade. It is about . . . let's see . . . two minutes after 5 a.m.—and we're counting on the fact that the bombing intensity slows up now. I hope I'm right."

Negotiations continued that morning with Jackson taking the lead and Blagojevich, with his knowledge of the language and his standing as a congressman, working the back channels with lower-level Serbian officials and religious leaders. The American delegation was also given a guided tour to view the damage done by NATO bombs. At noon Milosevic himself joined the negotiations. Much talking. Much disagreement. Little agreement. After three hours, Jackson and Milosevic left the room for a private stroll in the hotel's garden. At four o'clock in the afternoon Blagojevich and the rest of the delegation left the meeting room to catch up on much-needed sleep. There was still no deal to release the prisoners. Jackson made an urgent call to Washington, pleading for a halt in the bombing: "Don't set fire to this place tonight. This could stop everything." An hour later the phone in Jackson's hotel room rang again. Amazingly, the Milosevic forces told Jackson they would agree to release the three American prisoners the following morning.

Blagojevich and Jackson were not sure they could believe Milosevic, but they arrived at the designated government building earlier than the appointed hour the next morning. Papers were formally signed, and a quiet fell across the room. It was a stunning moment when a side door opened and the three American soldiers walked into the room. The three had been told only a short time earlier that they would be set free. They seemed bewildered by their sudden release.

They had entered the room with their heads down and their hands still clasped behind their back. Reverend Jackson approached them and said quietly, "Now that you are set free, let your first act be to take your hands from behind your backs because you're free and you can embrace." Slowly, their faces lit up. The feeling of all the Americans was one of jubilation as they left the building and boarded their bus for the long but joyous ride out of Serbia and a flight back to the United States.

Reverend Jesse Jackson received credit for the release of the three captured Americans, but Blagojevich was asked to accompany Jackson to the White House for a debriefing on their trip. Although the Clinton administration had strongly opposed the mission, they offered muted congratulations and listened to Jackson as he described the meetings with Milosevic. Jackson pushed the administration for a positive response to the release of the three prisoners with a matching gesture from the United States. And Congressman Blagojevich argued for a negotiated solution to the conflict, saying he was highly skeptical that the bombing campaign would succeed. But their pleas fell on deaf ears, and the bombing continued for another forty-one days before Milosevic agreed to a peace plan.

Back in Chicago, Dick Mell was delighted with the national and international coverage Blagojevich had received, even if he was seen mostly standing just behind Jesse Jackson. Chicago's Serbian community, however, was not so pleased with their congressman. They were angry—really angry—that Blagojevich, the only Serb in Congress, had not done more to stop the bombing. Desko Nikitovic, chairman of the Serbian Unity Congress of Illinois and a former politician in Serbia, had helped Blagojevich with many of the contacts for his Serbian trip. Afterward he declared that those Serbs who had lost family members in the NATO bombings were particularly upset with Blagojevich's lack of outrage over the war.

But Rod Blagojevich had bigger plans beyond representing the frustrations of Chicago's Serbs. The attention he had gained from his trip to Serbia had enhanced his visibility. He needed that to move up the political ladder, because Rod Blagojevich was ready to run for governor of Illinois.

6

The Race for Governor

WITH ONE of his favorite Elvis Presley CDs in the disk player and his always-present black oval hairbrush in the glove compartment, the candidate was upbeat as his SUV headed for the next campaign stop. Rod Blagojevich was on the road again, doing what he loved, getting out and mixing it up with the people. And he was enjoying a terrific response from voters as he plunged into appearances and handshaking throughout his twelve-hour day. It was early 2002, and Blagojevich was in the middle of a heated Democratic primary race for governor of Illinois, the nation's fifth-most-populous state. Chicagoans often think there's no Illinois outside the Windy City, but politicians running for statewide office know it's a very big state, some four hundred miles from north to south and a couple hundred miles wide. But geography didn't deter the gubernatorial wannabe. He was having the time of his life. At a church bingo tournament in a suburb southwest of Chicago, he wowed the crowd by tossing a $100 bill into the pot. Big round of applause for the handsome young candidate. And to cover all his bases, he tossed another $100 to the pinochle players on the other side of the hall. Clearly Blagojevich knew how to work a room.

"Whatever 'it' is, he's got it. Okay?" says his friend and former Springfield roommate Jay Hoffman. "When Rod goes into a room, people want to talk to him. People want to—believe it or not—want to come up and touch him, or shake his hand, or talk to him about issues."

Once he was back on the campaign trail, Blagojevich knew he had made the right decision to run for governor. Bored in Washington, he had eyed both the U.S. Senate seat and the governor's office. Mell told him he would help raise money for the governor's race, but he had no interest in helping him for a Senate seat. Mell wasn't interested in national politics where he would have little influence and no ability to gain jobs for his Thirty-third Warders.

Mell worried about Bill Daley's (Mayor Daley's brother) interest in running for governor. Daley was just coming off a successful stint as secretary of commerce in the Clinton administration and was ready to join the family business as a candidate himself. Hoping to clear the field for Blagojevich, Mell—according to Daley—tried to dirty him up by leaking stories about a possible conflict-of-interest problem while Daley had been an officer of the Amalgamated Bank in Chicago. The stories didn't gain much traction, but Bill Daley, who was going through a divorce, took himself out of the race, citing personal reasons.

Blagojevich's toughest Democratic primary opponent turned out to be Paul Vallas, the former superintendent of Chicago Public Schools. Vallas had received the credit—and probably deserved much of it—for the major turnaround of the city's troubled school system. The third candidate in the race for the biggest office in the statehouse, Roland Burris, was the first African American to be elected to a statewide office.

In 1979 Burris had begun the first of his three terms as state comptroller; he won statewide office again in 1991 when voters elected him Illinois attorney general. Initially Blagojevich thought he had neutralized some of Burris's black support because his congressional colleague, Jesse Jackson, Jr., had promised Blagojevich support. The two men had become friends. Both had young children and wives in Chicago, and they frequently traveled back and forth together. Jackson Jr. told Blagojevich he had more in common with him than he did with Burris and agreed to endorse him. But Jackson Jr. ran into a tougher reelection campaign than he had expected when political rivals put a seventy-one-year-old man named Jesse Jackson on the ballot. The Reverend Jesse Jackson Sr. told his son not to walk away from Burris and endorse a white man in the midst of his own difficult campaign. Jackson Jr. capitulated to his father and endorsed Burris. It was a betrayal Blagojevich never forgot.

It was ironic that, six years later, Blagojevich would select Burris, his old opponent for governor, to fill President Barack Obama's empty Senate seat after Blagojevich was arrested. And it was ironic that—after much objection and oratory from members of the Senate saying they would *never* seat the embattled governor's choice—Roland Burris became Illinois' junior senator. It wasn't a surprise, however, to those who knew Blagojevich, and could see that he had become a clever politician.

When Blagojevich and his father-in-law sought out David Axelrod to handle their campaign for governor, Axelrod turned down the work. He didn't think Blagojevich was ready to be governor. Blagojevich then hired Washington, D.C.–based Fred Yang of Garin Hart Yang for polling, and Bill Knapp from Squier Knapp Dunn for media. These two consultants would stay with Blagojevich for the rest of his career—and have often been accused of fueling his national ambitions at the expense of state politics.

For a campaign manager in 2002, Blagojevich turned to his old friend Lon Monk. Monk, who was in the midst of a new job in Washington with a financial services firm, was reluctant to enlist. "It was flattering, but I had just started this job, and I know *nothing* about politics." And Blagojevich said, "I *know* about politics. You don't need to know anything about *politics*, I need someone I can *trust* around me—and who has some management skills." So Monk came aboard.

Out on the political stump, Blagojevich promised to bring reform to a state that was all too familiar with political corruption. The incumbent governor, George Ryan, was on the brink of an indictment for corruption within his administration. Former governor Dan Walker had been an inmate at a Club Fed, as had Otto Kerner—all still within voters' memories. The people of Illinois were fed up with outlaw governors; they were ready for a reformer. Blagojevich vowed not to raise the state income tax, and he promised major changes in access to health care for families. He aimed his populist message "at the hard-working men and women in the state," often likening their struggles to those of his immigrant parents. In a state still reeling from corruption in the governor's office, young Rod Blagojevich was a fresh, new candidate, with a message that connected with the voters.

It was immediately clear to the candidates that downstate Illinois would be the key to a primary election victory. Both Blagojevich and Vallas were from Chicago. Burris was from downstate, Centralia. But as an African American, Burris's base came out of Chicago's black neighborhoods. Downstate was the only place left to all the candidates to pick up enough votes to make a difference. The campaign staff—the grizzled veterans of hard-fought Chicago campaigns and the fresh and idealistic new faces who came on board with the young candidate—was reluctant to have Dick Mell play a highly visible role in the campaign. But they knew they would have to count on him to bring in the other powerful Democratic chieftains in the city. Mell had more than a few victories under his belt, and he knew that he would have to do much more. He headed downstate to line up the Democratic party chairmen outside Chicago, men like Jerry Costello from Belleville and Jay Hoffman from Collinsville. These were the big players in statewide politics, the ones the new kids on the block knew nothing about. They were they ones who made victories happen.

When word of Mell's downstate wheeling and dealing surfaced, the campaign had its first whiff of trouble. Mell's involvement suggested to downstate voters a vision of a Blagojevich administration that smacked of Chicago patronage politics. "He's a Jacksonian Democrat," the *Springfield State Journal-Register* quoted Mell telling a group of downstate party chairmen about his candidate, ". . . not necessarily a *Jesse Jackson* Jacksonian, but an Andrew Jackson Jacksonian, who said 'to the victor belong the spoils.'" Rod Blagojevich took a big step back from his father-in law's statements at the time, though Mell's words would ultimately prove to be right on target.

The big players in Blagojevich's campaign for governor were good at fund-raising—very good. And because the campaign was flush with cash, it was able to flood the downstate airways with early campaign commercials. The ads stressed the Blagojevich campaign message—"opportunities for working people" and Blagojevich's immigrant roots: "My name is eastern European, my story is American." The campaign staff was particularly worried about the long ethnic name downstate. One downstate organizer, in an attempt to add a little humor to the dilemma, introduced the candidate as Rod "Bag-o-chips." But the long Serbian name proved to be less of a problem than anticipated. Maybe people couldn't say Blagojevich's name, but they could remember it as the name they couldn't pronounce.

The downstate early-media strategy paid off. Blagojevich squeaked out a primary win, gathering 37 percent of the vote with a strong downstate showing. Vallas came close with 34 percent while Burris won 29 percent.

In November Blagojevich employed the same strategy in the general election. His Republican opponent was Illinois attorney general Jim Ryan—who had the extreme misfortune to have the same last name as the beleaguered governor. A month after the primary election, U.S. Attorney Patrick Fitzgerald took an action that would almost guarantee Blagojevich a victory in the general election. The prosecutor filed a sweeping eighteen-count indictment against Governor George Ryan, alleging massive political corruption that led all the way to the governor's inner circle.

On the campaign trail, Rod Blagojevich hammered away at the corruption in the *Ryan* administration, an association that *Jim Ryan* could never escape. Even if he'd had a different name, Jim Ryan couldn't match Blagojevich's energy and charismatic campaign style. Blagojevich thrived on the campaign stump. Ryan never enjoyed plunging into crowds, shaking hands, or kissing babies. When his campaign staff pushed him out on the street one frigid October morning, Ryan lasted five minutes. He came back inside and told his advance man, "I got ten votes and double pneumonia."

But what gave Blagojevich the upper hand was the formidable amount of money flowing into his campaign. Most of the cash was due to the hustling of his chief fund-raiser, Christopher Kelly, a handsome, smooth-talking businessman from Chicago's southern suburbs. He had slicked-back hair and slick-looking suits—and a penchant for gambling. Like Blagojevich, Kelly was the son of working-class parents from downstate Champaign. He had come to the Chicago suburbs for high school but returned to his hometown to attend the University of Illinois. After graduating with a degree in landscape architecture, he went into business in the 1990s as a roofing contractor. His company thrived after he parlayed his friendship with insiders in the Daley administration into lucrative city contracts.

Kelly and Blagojevich met for the first time at a political fund-raiser in Chicago when both men were in their mid-thirties. By the time Blagojevich decided to run for governor, Chris Kelly had already made millions from his construction companies. He had a real head for business. But he also had a serious gambling problem that ultimately led to his downfall. In January 2009 Kelly pleaded guilty to income tax fraud, having used business funds to pay off more than $1 million in personal gambling debts. He admitted placing his bookie on the company payroll to help pay his debts. The next month he was reindicted on federal fraud and money-laundering charges in connection with alleged kickback schemes involving his roofing company and O'Hare International Airport.

In 2002, though, Kelly was riding high. He was bringing in so many cash contributions for the Blagojevich campaign chest that it caught the attention of a campaign finance watchdog group, the Illinois Campaign for Political Reform. The group's executive director, Cindi Canary, was stunned to see $650,000 in donations from four construction companies alone—all of them controlled by Kelly. Canary says those early contributions demonstrated a pattern of multiple, large, and coordinated contributions— all from affiliated businesses—to the governor's campaign fund. Just what were these heavy contributors expecting in return? Why was the candidate who was promising to root out political corruption in Illinois raising such huge sums of money from companies and contractors who did business with the state? Canary also wondered about a swap Kelly had orchestrated between the Blagojevich campaign and the Democratic Congressional Campaign Committee. More than $600,000 in campaign funds were shifted from a Blagojevich gubernatorial campaign account to the Democratic Congressional Campaign Committee—which then returned $900,000 in nonfederal money—"soft money'" in political language—to Blagojevich's gubernatorial campaign fund. Thus, money that had been donated to a federal election campaign was moved around and into a state campaign where different rules applied. It was all perfectly legal, though Cindi Canary's group found it troubling.

It took U.S. Attorney Patrick Fitzgerald three years to answer Cindi Canary's questions, and the answers weren't pretty. By 2005 the first indictments involving pay-to-play deals in the Blagojevich administration were announced.

But any warning storm clouds went unnoticed on election night, November 5, 2002. The Blagojevich campaign committee had rented a building in the North Side Finkl Steel complex. It was the mill where Rade Blagojevich had once worked, feeding the roaring blast furnaces. Some campaign workers worried that the big factory was *too* big—you never wanted to rent a place you couldn't fill. People would think your support wasn't deep, and they would doubt your political firepower.

Dick Mell, as always, was nervous. He watched as the vote totals trickled in. He had spent the entire day on the phone, talking to county chairmen, ward committeemen, and precinct captains, trying to get a sense of the voter turnout, trying to gauge whether this improbable victory of his son-in-law with the long, funny-sounding name, whose political career he had launched just ten years earlier, was really about to happen.

Blagojevich was upbeat and energized by the strong reception he had received on the campaign trail in the two weeks before election day. He told Mell to relax. The polls had showed Blagojevich and Ryan in a near dead heat two weeks earlier. But the tide had begun to shift and the numbers had been changing. On this election night, the politically connected of Chicago began to sense a victory. They got up from their TV sets and headed to the Blagojevich party. The enormous room began to fill—more than half full, then three-quarters. When the downstate precincts came in strong for Blagojevich, cheers rang out in the campaign boiler room where workers were watching the vote totals roll in. Hundreds, then thousands more poured into the hall and out into the streets. When two Chicago television stations projected Rod Blagojevich as the next governor of Illinois, a huge roar rose from the crowd. Balloons tumbled down around Rod and Patti, standing on the stage with four-year-old Amy in their arms.

Dick Mell turned to a friend standing next to him, leaned into the man's ear, and said, "He could be president."

7

Pay-to-Play on Steroids

ROD BLAGOJEVICH swept into office promising to clean out the stain of political corruption that had dogged the State of Illinois for decades. The good-looking young man from Chicago who would be the first Democratic governor in nearly a quarter-century vowed to open up state government to all of Illinois' citizens. A new energy permeated Springfield, with an expectation that an opportunity for real change was on the horizon.

Within months, however, the political pros closely watching the governor knew it wasn't about to happen. Like the cronies that preceded them, the inner circle that Blagojevich quickly put in place saw the new administration as full of opportunity—not for reform but for personal enrichment. Those figures closest to Governor Blagojevich were so blatantly corrupt that it took U.S. Attorney Patrick Fitzgerald only two and a half years to begin hammering down indictments.

When Blagojevich became governor, Fitzgerald's prosecutors were still hard at work, readying the corruption case against former governor George Ryan—Operation Safe Roads. When federal prosecutors launched a major new investigation into the Illinois governor's office—now run by Rod Blagojevich—they dubbed it "Operation Board Games."

It was Operation Board Games that led directly to the arrest of Governor Blagojevich on December 9, 2008. By the time Fitzgerald and the FBI put the handcuffs on the governor, the operation had already netted thirteen people, indicted or convicted in a corruption scheme that began the moment Rod Blagojevich stepped across the threshold and into the governor's office.

The key figure in the wide-ranging corruption that shattered the governor's office was Antoin "Tony" Rezko. An immigrant from Syria, Rezko had emigrated to the United States at age nineteen to further his engineering studies. Much like Rod Blagojevich's father, Rezko arrived in Chicago barely able to speak English and with few resources of his own. Yet within ten years his American dream was coming true. He had become a U.S. citizen, made a sizable fortune, and counted some of Chicago's biggest movers and shakers as his friends. A small, dapper man with a well-trimmed mustache, Rezko dressed well and lived elaborately. One journalist wrote that "he looked as though he had just stepped out of his tailor's shop after a trip to the barber." His sprawling, beautiful home in a wealthy suburb on Chicago's North Shore provided a breathtaking setting for the many fund-raisers he hosted for up-and-coming politicians, among them Barack Obama and Rod Blagojevich.

The association with Tony Rezko was one of the few bumps along Obama's road to the presidency. As a state senator he had purchased a piece of land next door to his new house in Chicago's Hyde Park neighborhood—a lot owned by Tony Rezko's wife. Obama told the *Washington Post* he regretted his actions, saying the purchase created the appearance that Tony Rezko did him a favor by selling him the lot. Obama admitted, "There's no doubt that this was a mistake on my part. 'Boneheaded' would be accurate. . . . I should have seen some red flags in terms of me purchasing a piece of property from him." Obama also donated to charity $11,500 that Rezko had contributed to his campaign.

For Governor Rod Blagojevich, the Rezko association was not a bump in the road, it was more like a fatal head-on crash. According to court testimony, Tony Rezko and Chris Kelly, the roofing contractor and consultant, took over Blagojevich's fund-raising operation well before he became governor. Early on the message was clear: if you wanted to "play" in a Blagojevich administration, you would have to "pay."

Ali Ata was one of those people who signed up to "play" early. Born in Jordan, Ata, like Rezko, had left the Middle East in his late teens to study engineering in America. With a bachelor's degree in engineering from the prestigious University of Illinois, he spent twenty-five years working for a water-treatment company in Naperville, Illinois, where he earned five U.S. patents. But his career was shattered when, two weeks after 9/11, the FBI came to his company to question him because of the unfortunate similarity of his name to a 9/11 hijacker, Mohamed Atta. No connection or relationship was ever found, but despite his five patents and years of service, the company forced Ata out with an early retirement.

Ata then decided he had the ability to make a go in the real estate business. He had Middle Eastern good looks, beautiful skin and teeth, dark hair just brushed with a little grey. He dressed attractively in tweeds and sports coats, though never as expensively as his friend Rezko. His appearance was that of an intellectual. But he was highly successful, piling up considerable wealth with a shrewd eye for real estate development. That's where he met Tony Rezko. He also crossed paths with Dick Mell and became an early supporter of Rod Blagojevich's political career. Ata was one of the first people Blagojevich turned to for support after deciding to run for governor in 2002, and he responded gladly by hosting two fund-raisers early that year.

As Blagojevich's chances of beating Jim Ryan grew, Ali Ata began thinking about asking for a position in a Blagojevich administration. Ata's real estate deals had made him rich, so it wasn't necessarily a big salary he was after. But he did have dreams of being the highest-ranking Muslim in the Blagojevich administration. The man to see about it, he knew, was his friend Tony Rezko.

Ali Ata eventually testified that he arranged a meeting at Rezko's North Side office two months before the gubernatorial election in 2002. Blagojevich would be there, Rezko assured him. Ata should come—and bring a check, a big one. Ushered into the outer office by Rezko, Ata shook his hand, then handed him a check for $25,000. Sure enough, Blagojevich was there, waiting in the inner office along with Chris Kelly, Lon Monk, and State Representative Jay Hoffman. This was the core of what became known as Blagojevich's "kitchen cabinet." Kelly, Monk, and Hoffman stepped over into an isolated corner of the room and began talking among themselves as Ali Ata sat down facing the candidate. Tony Rezko was at Blagojevich's right hand; Ata's $25,000 check lay in the middle of the table. The three men exchanged small talk about the progress of the campaign, and Blagojevich thanked Ata for being a supporter and a team player. Rezko now told the future governor that Ata was interested in serving in his administration. Blagojevich asked if Ata knew what position might be of interest to him. Rezko replied that indeed he did. Ata had done his homework, searching the Illinois state government website, and had found three positions he might like. He had given his list to Rezko before the meeting. Ata had his eye on the Capitol Development Board, the Department of Transportation, and the Department of Human Services.

Just one day after Rod Blagojevich took his oath as the forty-second governor of Illinois, Rezko called Ata and told him he would become the next executive director of the Capitol Development Board, the construction management arm of Illinois government. Ata was delighted. But three months later he had not yet been appointed to the position. He found out why when he went back to Rezko to see what was going on. Rezko told him he had just gotten off the phone with Jay Hoffman, who had screamed at him for making a promise he couldn't deliver. Hoffman told him the Capitol Development Board position had already been given to someone from downstate. And, Hoffman had said, that was the way it was going to stay.

Another three months passed before Rezko called Ata back into his office to reveal the possibility of another state job. Five of the state agencies dealing with finance were about to be consolidated into a new agency, the Illinois

Finance Authority. The governor, Rezko said, was offering Ata a position as executive director of the new agency. But, he said, Ata must make another campaign contribution, this time for $50,000. Ata told Rezko he could not come up with $50,000, but he could get another $25,000.

With a second $25,000 check in hand, Ali Ata showed up at the governor's spring fund-raiser, a very crowded event on Navy Pier. As Chicago's most-frequented tourist destination, Navy Pier is a beautiful rehabilitation of restaurants, galleries, and activities. It juts out into Lake Michigan where the Chicago River meets the lake with all of downtown Chicago glittering just across the way. With the giant Ferris wheel slowly circling in the soft night sky and lights on the pier twinkling, Ata handed his second check to Tony Rezko. A few minutes later Governor Blagojevich waved Ata over to his side. He thanked Ata for his support and told him he was aware of the new check. In his testimony Ata told federal prosecutors that Blagojevich "understood that I was considering a position with a new administration and said it better be a job where I can make some money." Apparently Ata had paid the price of admission.

Six months later, in October 2003, Ata was formally offered the position of executive director of the Illinois Finance Authority. He began work in January 2004, when the Authority was up and running. But there was a catch: Rezko, who no had position with the State of Illinois, made it clear to Ali Ata that it was he, Tony Rezko, who would control the Finance Authority. Rezko told Ata that if he wanted the job, he must agree to report to Rezko at least weekly. Ata agreed. He set up the meetings through Rezko's secretary.

The indictments and convictions in Patrick Fitzgerald's Operation Board Games would eventually show that controlling the state boards and agencies was at the heart of the corruption in the first term of the Blagojevich administration. The Illinois Finance Authority was just one of the state offices that Rezko and Chris Kelly sought to control. They already had a hand in two other boards through Stuart Levine, a holdover appointee from the George Ryan administration. Levine was a lifelong Republican, but he loved the game—and just now the game was being played by Democrats. Stuart Levine had in fact been campaign finance chairman in Jim Ryan's unsuccessful run against Blagojevich. Now in his early sixties, he had contributed more than $1.3 million to Republican candidates from 1993 to 2002. Initially he had made his money as a founder of HMO America, which owned and operated the largest health maintenance organization in Illinois. He served on numerous boards and charitable organizations and was a major contributor and fund-raiser for the Jewish United Fund and other Jewish organizations.

A distinguished-looking man with greying hair and rimless glasses, Levine dressed impeccably and traveled in the highest social circles. He had been knighted by the king of Sweden for furthering a better relationship between Sweden and the United States. To all who knew him, Stuart Levine was the perfect picture of the successful Republican businessman with a loving wife and two beautiful children. But when things blew up in his face, federal court testimony revealed some dark secrets about the man. His colleagues were stunned to learn that Levine frequented male prostitutes and paid for all-night sex parties at a suburban hotel nicknamed for its garish paint job, the Purple Hotel. (The hotel had its own shady past, from a grisly 1983 Chicago mob hit in the hotel parking lot.)

Apparently a serious drug addiction was at the root of Levine's behavior. He admitted to thirty years of drug use, telling prosecutors that from 2002 to 2004 he had spent more than a million dollars on an astonishing variety of drugs, ranging from LSD to cocaine, crystal methamphetamine, and even an animal tranquilizer known as ketamine which produces euphoria in humans. Levine used the drugs to fuel all-night sex parties both in Springfield and Chicago. But apparently he was able to function well enough to hide his underground lifestyle from his wife of thirty-three years and his two children. Stuart Levine testified that he had never brought drugs into his family's luxurious lakefront home in a wealthy North Shore suburb. Nor did his secret life seem to interfere with his extensive business dealings with the state.

Levine had been appointed by Governor George Ryan to a seat on the Teachers' Retirement System Board (TRS), the state's pension plan for teachers and administrators. The TRS had 325,000 members and assets in excess of $30 billion. Levine also served on the Illinois Health Facilities Planning Board, responsible for reviewing new projects for health-care facilities.

When Democrat Blagojevich won the governor's office, Levine wanted to keep his seat on the two influential boards, so he went to the man who could make it happen, Tony Rezko. Soon Blagojevich reappointed Levine to both positions. When questioned about why he had appointed Republican Levine, Blagojevich's spokesman, Abby Ottenhoff, told members of the media the governor reappointed Levine to the Health Facilities Planning Board because it required a Republican member. And, she said, he reappointed Levine to the TRS as an "olive branch, really showing his intention to work in a bipartisan way."

With Levine's board positions secured, Rezko and Levine devised the plans that would dominate Blagojevich's term as governor. They did so at a quiet dinner at the prestigious, members-only Standard Club, just down the street from the U.S. attorney's office in Chicago's Loop. Over prime strip steaks and vintage red wine, Levine told Rezko that their relationship with the governor could be worth as much $3.9 million to Rezko alone. Quite a bit of their scam was already working well. Businesses dealing with the state boards and commissions were told to hire *consultants* or favored *contractors*. These consultants and contractors, who were in on the deal, would kick back money to Rezko and Levine, and to the governor's campaign fund. And these were not just a few dollars but enormous sums of money—at least $7 million from scams involving the TRS board and another $1 to $2 million from deals relating to the Health Facilities Planning Board. The Levine-Rezko scheme was eventually uncovered by Patrick Fitzgerald, who dubbed it "pay-to-play on steroids."

Patrick Fitzgerald may never have learned of these schemes had it not been for a gentle-speaking, blonde, suburban mother of three children who, fed up with the corruption she saw around her, agreed to wear a wire for the FBI. Pamela Meyer Davis was the CEO of Edward, a large hospital complex in Naperville, Illinois. To keep up with the burgeoning population of Naperville, one of the fastest-growing areas in the country, the hospital had doubled in size over a twenty-year period. But Meyer Davis, who had led the hospital for all of those twenty years, was well aware that the hospital needed to continue to grow. Thus in 2003 she initiated an application for expansion to the Illinois Health Facilities Planning Board. Stuart Levine was a member of that board, and he and Tony Rezko had also arranged the appointment of two other board members. These were votes they could count on for sure. One of those members was Dr. Imad Alamanseer, a pathologist with longtime ties to Rezko. In his later court testimony, Alamanseer recounted that he was ordered to watch Stuart Levine's votes during Planning Board meetings, and then to vote the same way because "that's how Tony [Rezko] wants it."

Pamela Meyer Davis didn't suspect that she was up against a stacked board when Edward Hospital made its initial application for expansion. But she soon sensed that something was strange about the process. A day or two before the board was set to vote on Edward's application, a business acquaintance of Meyer Davis, Nicholas Hurtgen, who was the managing director of the investment firm Bear Stearns, called her at home. He told her she would have to use a certain contractor or else the Health Facilities Board would turn down the hospital's request for expansion. Filled with disbelief, she ignored the warning and went to the board meeting expecting clearance to expand. Imagine her shock when the Edward Hospital's $115 million expansion plan was turned down flat. "I was humiliated," Meyer Davis told the *New Yorker* magazine. "They were mean. So I walk off, and then a different guy comes up to me and he says, 'We told you to pull your project. Call me.' And right then I decided to call the FBI."

At first the FBI showed little interest in the complaint of a suburban hospital administrator. But Meyer Davis wouldn't quit until the feds agreed she might have a genuine complaint. They came to the hospital, planted bugs in her office, and showed her how to wear a tiny tape recorder in her bra.

Meyer Davis then phoned Hurtgen and the contractor he wanted her to use, Jacob Kiferbaum, to arrange a meeting in her office at the hospital. FBI agents were staked out in a nondescript van in the hospital's garage, listening to the recorded conversation that was also being transmitted to them. It didn't take long for the FBI to become *very* interested. As Hurtgen and Kiferbaum spoke, the microphone picked up their words clearly: "We told you to pull the project. If you don't hire us, you will *never* get this project approved."

Immediately Meyer Davis's phone began to ring. It was the three FBI agents in the garage yelling that they had what they needed. "It's extortion! It's extortion! Get them out!" Awkwardly, she dreamed up a story about a family emergency and quickly rushed the men out of her office.

That conversation, recorded by FBI agents in Meyer Davis's Naperville office, was the official beginning of U.S. Attorney Patrick Fitzgerald's Operation Board Games. An application for hospital expansion in a suburb on the fringe of Chicago, denied by a tainted board, was the first step along the road to the arrest of Governor Rod Blagojevich.

For Meyer Davis, it wasn't a simple process. For eight months she wore a tiny tape recorder in her bra whenever she met with Hurtgen, Kiferbaum, and other crooked contractors in bars and upscale restaurants around Chicago. She spent hours listening—and taping—as the men described their plans to rip off the state. It was a bizarre cloak-and-dagger role for Meyer Davis, who had always prided herself on running an open hospital administration. Now she found herself sneaking around, driving in to downtown Chicago to drop off her covert tape-recorded conversations for FBI pickup at the cosmetics counter of a large department store. Although she taped a wide variety of incriminating conversations, she told the media she never quite got used to being a spy. "The wire is a little tiny square thing I put inside my bra. I thought it would fall out all the time," she said. "Oh, the logistics of getting the stuff done. One morning I had to meet one of the FBI guys in my office at 6 a.m., so he could hook up a wire to tap my phone. He was under my desk, on the floor. It looks kinky! My administrative assistant pops her head in, and there's this man under my desk, and she says, 'Oh, my goodness!' and leaves. And I say, 'What am I supposed to tell her?' He says, 'I don't know. That's never happened to me before.'"

At one point the "bad guys," as Meyer Davis called them, advised her she could win approval for the Edward Hospital expansion plan if she were to sign a construction contract with Kiferbaum, which she knew was padded by several million dollars. The FBI wanted her to sign, but she refused, fearing she might endanger the hospital. Her cover was blown seven months later when the *Chicago Sun-Times* published her name in a story about an ongoing corruption investigation.

Pamela Meyer Davis never did get her expansion plan approved by the Health Facilities Board. But another Chicago area hospital, Mercy, did gain approval to build a new hospital in north suburban Crystal Lake. Federal court testimony leaves little doubt that "pay to play" was behind the approval. The first time Mercy Hospital applied for permission to expand, in December 2003, the hospital was turned down. Levine told Kiferbaum he would get the board to approve Mercy's application, but he stipulated that it would cost Kiferbaum if he wanted the contract to build the hospital. Kiferbaum agreed to pay a kickback in order to get the job but didn't agree to an exact figure. Levine thereupon told Rezko, who in turn agreed to direct his appointees on the board to support the Mercy expansion plan in exchange for a share of Kiferbaum's kickback. They set the kickback fee at approximately $1 million.

The Health Facilities Board meeting for the Mercy Hospital application was set for April 21, 2003. Levine was nervous, unsure how the board's chairman, Thomas Beck, would vote. (Beck was attempting to maintain a measure of independence.) Undoubtedly Levine would have been more nervous if he had known the FBI was taping his conversations with Beck. Two nights before the meeting, the tapes disclose Levine telling Beck, "I got the marching orders . . . there's one—I think you may be able to help us—Mercy Hospital. Our boy wants to help them." *Our boy* was Tony Rezko, who now had a strong interest in pushing the deal through. But Beck wasn't convinced, and he still planned to vote "no."

Levine was also concerned about another board member Rezko was counting on, Dr. Imad Alamanseer, the respected pathologist at a large suburban hospital. At the time of his appointment, Rezko owed Alamanseer half a million dollars on a loan that Alamanseer had given him to shore up his ailing Papa John's Pizza and Panda Express franchises. Despite his arrangements with Rezko, Dr. Alamanseer took his planning board responsibilities seriously and had spent long hours studying the $81 million Mercy Hospital building plan. He was concerned about a more equitable distribution of health-care facilities for the Crystal Lake area. He was prepared to vote against the Mercy application, just as he had at the December meeting after watching Levine.

Just before the meeting began, a call came through from Rezko. In court Beck said he told Rezko, "Tony, this just isn't a good application. Take this job and shove it. I'll resign."

Rezko replied, "Do what you have to do."

Beck told the federal jury, "I took it to mean, 'Get it approved.'"

Dr. Alamanseer got the message too. Although he testified that he was "disgusted and humiliated" by the pressure he felt from Rezko and Levine, he voted to approve the project.

Beck too had second thoughts. He decided he liked being chairman of the Illinois Health Facilities Planning Board. He voted "yes" and kept his job.

8

The Way It's Done in Illinois

THE GREED of Rezko, Levine, and others in the Blagojevich inner circle was driven by the availability of billions of dollars in state funds with little oversight. These could be used to build the governor's campaign coffers for his second-term run as well as to enrich themselves. But those closest to the governor—Tony Rezko especially— also believed that Rod Blagojevich, the handsome, Elvis-loving, first-generation Serbian-American Democrat from Chicago, had a real chance to become President of the United States of America. And money would help.

Blagojevich himself dreamed of running for president. Those dreams were not unrealistic. At age forty-six he had become governor of the fifth-largest state in the nation after a successful populist campaign. Voters responded to his upbeat, energetic campaign style. And, of substantial importance, he had pulled in an unprecedented amount of campaign cash. He had also gained the support of many of his Democratic colleagues after winning the governor's office. In 2003 Chicago Congresswoman Jan Schakowsky and Congressman William Lipinksi both said they wouldn't be at all surprised if Blagojevich was contemplating a presidential run.

To campaign for president, Blagojevich knew he would have to have an even more sophisticated fund-raising operation than the one that brought him the governorship. He saw the opportunity to upgrade when he met the man who had been Al Gore's top fund-raiser in his 2000 campaign for the presidency. Joe Cari was a successful corporate lawyer in Chicago, with credentials as an ally to Mayor Richard J. Daley, a high-flying law degree from the University of Notre Dame, and battle scars from working Democratic campaigns around Chicago. A tall, attractive man with dark wavy hair that spoke of his Italian heritage, Cari radiated success in his expensive Italian suits and ties. He particularly loved the dark-pinstripe-with-pastel-tie look and wore it often. Cari had connections to all the best political names, from Jimmy Carter to Bill Clinton and Joe Biden. He had been involved as a fund-raiser and strategist in every presidential campaign since Walter Mondale's in 1980, and he'd held a number of important appointments by the Democratic National Committee.

The son of a prominent physician, Cari had grown up in the southwest Chicago suburb of Evergreen Park. He came into the city to attend Brother Rice High School, where he excelled academically and as an athlete, playing baseball and basketball. He chose the University of Notre Dame for both college and law school, then plunged immediately into national politics, landing a job as counsel to President Jimmy Carter's reelection campaign in Illinois. Four years later that job expanded to counsel for

Walter Mondale's Midwest presidential effort. Cari joined a prominent downtown Chicago law firm but kept his hand in national Democratic politics. He raised big money for the presidential runs of Joe Biden, Bob Kerrey, Bill Clinton, John Kerry, and Al Gore. He was sought out as an astute political strategist and was even tapped by Harvard University in 2002 to teach a course on the financial aspects of presidential campaigns.

Over the years Cari served on a number of boards, and in 1995 President Clinton appointed him to the board of the Woodrow Wilson International Center for Scholars in Washington. The board was star-studded with political and policy heavyweights—interesting and challenging for the brilliant lawyer. It was this appointment, however, that led Joe Cari to cross paths with U.S. Attorney Patrick Fitzgerald.

On the Wilson Center board Cari met John H. Foster, a financial entrepreneur who persuaded Cari to join in establishing a new private equity firm. The idea was to solicit money from state pension funds to invest in the lucrative orthopedic device industry. Cari could see the possibilities, and so it was that HealthPoint Capital was born. While George Ryan was still governor of Illinois, Cari began looking at the Illinois Teachers' Retirement System fund, TRS, with its $30 billion in assets, as a good source of business. In late 2002, Cari made a pitch to TRS.

Not long after, Cari met Stuart Levine at a political fund-raiser for Jim Ryan, Blagojevich's Republican opponent for governor. The event was hosted by Cari's law firm. Joe Cari had never supported a Republican candidate in his life, but he was making an exception for Ryan because of a tragic personal event. Cari's wife, Rita Bahr, had lost a battle with cancer earlier that year at the young age of forty-four. By every account Joe and Rita's marriage—a second for both of them—had been a dream come true. Even as Rita's cancer worsened, the two lovers traveled the world together, squeezing as much joy as possible into whatever time they had left together. Their last year became more and more difficult as Rita's cancer spread to her brain. Surprisingly, both Joe and Rita found some comfort from a man they barely knew, Jim Ryan, who had survived his own battle with cancer. They became friends with Ryan and his wife, who spent many hours with Rita and Joe in their home, encouraging and supporting them.

That's how Cari found himself making his first major contribution to a Republican, giving $3,666 to Jim Ryan for the governor's race. In another first, Cari gave *no money* to the Democratic candidate for governor, Rod Blagojevich. "I was a little bit astounded because [Cari] was a high-ranking Democratic official," Ryan told a reporter. "But I think honestly it was a personal thing, and he kind of told that to me, that some things are more important than politics." The friendship continued up to and beyond Rita Bahr's death.

Even though he knew it was coming, the loss of his wife devastated Joe Cari. He lost interest in politics and battled depression for several years. Hoping to lure him back into the political scene and into life in general, a good friend, David Wilhelm, the former chairman of the Democratic National Committee and a pallbearer at Rita Bahr's funeral, began talking to Cari about Blagojevich in the summer of 2003. Wilhelm had served as head of the Blagojevich transition team. He knew Cari had supported Jim Ryan, but he wanted Cari's expertise on board for the Blagojevich administration. Wilhelm too thought Blagojevich had possibilities as a presidential candidate, and he wanted Cari to help them lay out a national fund-raising strategy. But Cari wasn't interested. He told Wilhelm that the loss of his wife was still too painful for him, that he just didn't have the energy or the will to return to politics. To placate Wilhelm, Cari agreed to meet with Tony Rezko and Chris Kelly. But he turned down their pleas for help with national fund-raising for Blagojevich.

Cari did maintain his relationship with Stuart Levine, which was initially quite productive—though ultimately it would lead to Cari's downfall. With Levine's help as a TRS board member, the teachers' pension fund agreed to two investments with HealthPoint Capital for a total of $35 million.

By October 2003, Cari had softened in his reluctance to raise funds for Blagojevich and agreed to arrange a fund-raiser in New York City which HealthPoint would host. The event was to be the first effort for a possible presidential run. Stuart Levine would pick up the $4,000 tab for the private plane to New York. On the morning of October 29 Governor Blagojevich, Stuart Levine, Chris Kelly, and two others close to Blagojevich, John Wyma and Bradley Tusk, boarded the plane along with Joe Cari. In describing the trip to the jury in his political corruption trial, Cari said he was asked by Tusk, Blagojevich's chief of staff, to switch seats with him and sit next to Blagojevich. For the next thirty minutes Blagojevich talked to Cari about his presidential aspirations. The governor wanted to learn all he could from Cari's fund-raising experiences. Blagojevich talked of Clinton and his success as president, telling Cari why he thought a sitting governor was in a good position to raise campaign cash. "The governor," Cari said Blagojevich told him, "has the ability, unlike a U.S. senator, to give contracts, legal work, advisory work, consulting work, investment banking work to a variety of individuals and companies." That made it much easier, Blagojevich told Cari, "to solicit people for contributions." Blagojevich told Cari how much he liked and respected Tony Rezko and Chris Kelly, the two people he trusted most, the key people in his administration. He also made a strong pitch to Cari for his help in putting together the governor's national fund-raising strategy for a presidential run, telling Cari there was investment banking work and consulting work available to people who helped them.

Cari testified that he was a bit stunned by the governor's blunt conversation. But he again turned down Blagojevich's pleas, saying, "I was having a very difficult time going on with my life. I had taken a lot of time off. I just wasn't in a position to do the kinds of things that I think the governor was looking for me to do."

Later at the fund-raiser at the posh Harvard Club in New York, Stuart Levine once more laid out the fund-raising strategy for Cari. According to Cari, Levine told him, "There was going to be consultants and lawyers and investment bankers that would be picked by the administration or people around the administration; and that those people then would be in return solicited for political contributions. It was also told to me that the people around the governor would pick consultants who wanted to do business—consultants for companies who wanted to do business with a variety of the state boards; and that eventually the Blagojevich administration would have control of all of the state boards."

From January to March 2004 Rezko, Levine, and Kelly continue to wine and dine Cari, hoping to persuade him to come aboard as their national fund-raiser. In a small café just west of downtown Chicago in March, Kelly again pushed Cari hard, offering him whatever he wanted—legal work, more investment in his private equity firm, consulting work, a seat on a state board—if he would only put together a fund-raising plan for Blagojevich. Again Cari declined, but he was about to be caught up in the very money-raising scheme that Kelly, Levin, and Rezko had laid out to him.

Cari continued to stay in touch with Levine about possible investment business for HealthPoint from the State of Illinois. Levine told him there was little more he could get from the TRS fund, but he would look into the Illinois State Board of Investments (ISBI), which handled the pension assets of the retirement systems of the General Assembly, state judges, and Ilinois state employees. But Levine made it clear that a consultant or "finder" picked by Rezko or Levine would have to be hired and paid a percentage of the investment for any deal to go through. Levine was looking for 2 percent on a $35 million ISBI deal, which would mean a finder's fee of $700,000. Cari understood that fee would then be kicked back through Rezko, with some ending up in the governor's campaign coffers, but he reluctantly agreed.

Unbeknownst to Cari, his partner in HealthPoint, Carl McCall, was also dealing with Levine—but on behalf of another investment firm, J. E. Roberts. J. E. Roberts had been very helpful to McCall when he had run for governor of New York, and he wanted to see if Levine could help push through an $85 million investment that Roberts hoped to secure from the teachers' retirement fund. Cari learned about McCall's efforts with TRS when Levine called to tell him he had picked a consultant whom J. E. Roberts would have to use to get the deal. Levine thus hoped to apply more pressure to Cari.

After Cari returned home from a trip to the Far East, he had increasingly heated conversations with Levine about J. E. Roberts' failure to hire the consultant Rezko had named, or to convey the $850,000 finder's fee prescribed for the $85 million deal. With the TRS May board meeting fast approaching, Cari made a series of phone calls to J. E. Roberts, whose president turned out to be the daughter of a good friend of Cari's from the Clinton administration. Deborah Harmon's father, James A. Harmon, an international financier, had been appointed by Clinton to be chairman and president of the U.S. Export-Import Bank.

Deborah Harmon told Cari she knew who he was, but she was concerned about the pressure J. E. Roberts was getting to pay an $850,000 finder's fee to a consultant the firm had never heard of. The consulting contract, Harmon's lawyer said, had been faxed to the J. E. Roberts office from an unknown firm in the Turks and Caicos Islands in the Caribbean. In court testimony Cari says he told Harmon, "In Illinois people around the governor pick the consultants, law firms, investment banking firms; and that this has been the history of Illinois; and that this is the way it's done in Illinois." And Cari again insisted that unless the sham consulting contract was signed, the $85 million deal would be dead. Deborah Harmon stuck to her guns and refused to sign the contract.

But something else happened on May 20, 2004, the same day Cari was talking with Harmon: the FBI made its first contact with Stuart Levine. Shaken, Levine backed off at the TRS board meeting five days later and J. E. Roberts got its $85 million investment without a finder's fee.

Levine was also feeling heat from Thomas Rosenberg, another principal in an investment firm. Rosenberg, a Chicago businessman turned Hollywood movie producer best known for his movie *Million Dollar Baby*, was trying to glean $220 million from the teachers' pension fund for his investment firm Capri Capitol. According to secret FBI tapes and Rosenberg's testimony in federal court, Capri had been turned down by the TRS board in February 2004. Angered, he had then called longtime Republican operative William Cellini, who was now dealing with the Blagojevich administration. Cellini informed Rosenberg that Capri had lost the TRS investment money because he hadn't used a consultant or a finder and hadn't contributed to the Blagojevich campaign fund. But, said Cellini, the deal could still go through if Rosenberg agreed to pay a $2 million fee to a consultant chosen by Rezko and Levine, or make a $1.5 million campaign contribution. Now furious, Rosenberg told Cellini that he would not be extorted. Rosenberg testified, "I told him that I wouldn't give them a dime. . . . I told Cellini I would tell this story on the corner of State and Madison. . . . I told them, if there wasn't a grand jury in session against Rezko and Kelly, that there shortly will be."

Rosenberg's threat to go to the feds prompted a flurry of phone calls among Rezko, Levine, Kelly, and Cellini. Worried about what Rosenberg might do, Levine told the group it was too risky to continue demanding that Rosenberg pay up. They should allow his investment deal to go through at the upcoming May 25 board meeting.

But the group agreed that it would be the last investment deal Rosenberg got from TRS.

In a phone call the following day, Rezko, according to court testimony, told Levine that he had talked to Blagojevich, who agreed with the plan to cut Rosenberg out of future state pension deals. "The governor indicated he doesn't care what happens to Mr. Rosenberg. He feels he owes Mr. Rosenberg nothing."

In retrospect, it's clear that by the May 25 TRS board meeting, Patrick Fitzgerald's Operation Board Games investigation was well on the way to its first indictment. It would take another year, but on May 9, 2005, Stuart Levine and Jacob Kiferbaum were indicted on a variety of corruption charges, including demanding kickbacks from applicants to the Illinois Health Facilities Planning Board. Four months later Levine and Joseph Cari were indicted for attempting to extort money from investment firms seeking business from the Illinois Teachers Retirement System's pension fund. Kiferbaum and Cari both entered guilty pleas and began cooperating with the government late in 2005. One year later, on October 11, 2006, Fitzgerald reeled in the biggest fish in his Operation Board Games campaign, Antoin "Tony" Rezko. The twenty-four-count superseding indictment also included Stuart Levine.

At the news conference announcing the indictment, Fitzgerald explained, "This indictment describes a frenzy of corrupt scheming, particularly in April and May of 2004, in which political insiders sought to manipulate the activities of two state boards to fleece investment firms and individuals. The defendants and their associates put the word out loud and clear: you have to pay to play in

Illinois." Within two weeks Stuart Levine pled guilty and began cooperating with the government.

Next it was Chris Kelly's turn to be caught up in Fitzgerald's probe. In December 2007 he faced indictment not for his dealings in the Blagojevich administration but for federal tax fraud charges—using corporate funds to cover gambling debts he had run up in Las Vegas and with a local bookie. Kelly pled guilty in January 2009. He was reindicted one month later on fraud charges related to roofing contracts at O'Hare Airport. William Cellini became the thirteenth defendant charged in Operation Board Games with his indictment on October 30, 2008.

But before that, in March 2008, Patrick Fitzgerald's prosecutors began the biggest political corruption trial in Illinois since the conviction of former Governor George Ryan two years earlier. At the three-month trial of Tony Rezko, jurors heard testimony from Stuart Levine, Chris Kelly, Ali Ata, Joseph Cari, and Thomas Rosenberg, among many others. On June 5, 2008, Rezko was found guilty on sixteen of twenty–four counts. Fitzgerald called the verdict a warning to Illinois politicians: "I hope people step back and say, 'When you do all that stuff, it's going to come back and bite you in a serious way.' If the morals don't get to them, then I hope the fear of going to jail does."

But the state's highest-ranking official didn't seem to get the message. Patrick Fitzgerald continued to build his case against Rod Blagojevich right up to the moment the FBI showed up on the governor's doorstep on that cold December morning to tell the governor he was under arrest.

U.S. Attorney Patrick Fitzgerald, the aggressive
and indefatigable chief prosecutor in the political
corruption case against impeached Illinois
governor Rod Blagojevich.

Illinois governor Otto Kerner, shown in 1967 with New York mayor John Lindsay. Kerner was convicted of seventeen counts of bribery, conspiracy, perjury, and related charges in 1974 and served eight months of a three-year sentence in a federal prison.

Illinois governor Dan Walker pled guilty to bank fraud, misapplication of bank funds, and perjury in 1987 and served eighteen months of a seven-year sentence in a federal prison.

Illinois governor George Ryan is swarmed by the media after his conviction on racketeering and fraud charges on April 17, 2006.

Richard J. Daley, first elected mayor of Chicago in 1955, set a standard for effective urban political organizations in America—and managed to keep his nose clean.

In 1989 Richard M. Daley succeeded to the office his father had held; he was reelected to an unprecedented sixth term in 2007. The younger Daley has governed with less reliance on party organization.

Young Rod Blagojevich winks after losing a Golden Gloves fight in
1975.

Alderman Dick Mell looks on as his son-
in-law waves during his inauguration as
governor of Illinois in January 2003.

Rod Blagojevich jogs past the Old State Capitol in Springfield the day before his inauguration in 2003.

House Speaker Michael Madigan, Governor Blagojevich's longtime nemesis, shakes hands before the governor's budget address in February 2004.

Blagojevich announces for a second term as governor with his wife Patti by his side in February 2006.

Antoin "Tony" Rezko was convicted on sixteen counts of mail fraud, bribery, and money laundering in June 2008. He had used political clout to orchestrate a multi-million-dollar kickback scheme in the Blagojevich administration.

Stuart Levine, center, pled guilty in October 2007 to using his seats on two state boards to collect millions of dollars in kickbacks, some of which found their way into Governor Blagojevich's campaign coffers. He was sentenced to sixty-seven months in prison after agreeing to cooperate with the government.

Governor Blagojevich
faces the media the day
his top fund-raiser and
close confidant Tony
Rezko was convicted.
Blagojevich denied
any knowledge of the
corruption.

Roland Burris in an expansive mood on December 30, 2008, just
after Governor Blagojevich announced that Burris was his choice to
fill the vacant Senate seat of Barack Obama.

9

New Man in Springfield

ILLINOIS DEMOCRATS could not have foreseen how badly things would end for Rod Blagojevich when he was sworn in on January 13, 2003. Democrats were elated to have won not only control of the governor's office but both houses of the legislature. Voters had bought candidate Blagojevich's Democratic message offering a new era of reform after the departure of the scandal-laden administration of Governor George Ryan. But scattered among this new administration were the seeds of corruption that would eventually bring down Rod Blagojevich.

Right from the start, the Democratic governor had a problem with the Democratic House of Representatives, and particularly with its leader, Michael Madigan. In 2002 Mike Madigan was considered by most observers to be the most powerful Democrat in the state, next to Chicago mayor Richard M. Daley. In state politics for nearly four decades, Madigan's base is in the southwest side of Chicago—the Thirteenth Ward, once solidly white and ethnic, mostly Irish and Polish. Over the years it has become heavily Latino with some African Americans, though large numbers of white ethnic city workers, police officers, firefighters, and teachers still live in the classic small Chicago bungalows that line the neighborhood's streets. Madigan's powerful Thirteenth Ward Democratic organization has historically been among the most effective in the city, rivaling those of the Eleventh Ward, home of the Daley family, and Dick Mell's Thirty-third Ward.

Born in 1942, the slightly built Madigan is Irish to the bone. His red hair and fair skin give away his Hibernian heritage. He is a tightly wound, disciplined man, who appreciates order and tolerates little dissent. A lifelong Chicagoan, Madigan attended what many consider to be the most prestigious Catholic high school in the city, St. Ignatius, then continued his Catholic education at the University of Notre Dame and Loyola University Law School. Not long after winning his law degree, he was elected to his first term as a state representative in 1971. That same year he was a delegate to the Illinois Constitutional Convention in Springfield, which drew up the rules used in Governor Blagojevich's impeachment trial thirty-eight years later.

In 1982 Madigan won the powerful position of speaker of the Illinois House, and except for a brief two-year period when Republicans gained control of the House, he has wielded the gavel of the speaker ever since. He added to the Illinois tradition of powerful political families when he helped elect his adopted daughter, Lisa Madigan, first a state senator and then Illinois attorney general.

Madigan's other major responsibility has been the chairmanship of the Illinois Democratic party. In that role he supported his daughter for attorney general and Rod

Blagojevich for governor in the November 2002 election. And it was in that gubernatorial contest that Mike Madigan gave Blagojevich an early warning, a sign of things to come. It occurred at Democrat Day at the Illinois State Fair in Springfield, when Democratic candidates and officeholders from around the state come to the fair to shake hands and eat corn on the cob and anything else that can be fried and put on a stick. It's a day to rev up the Democratic troops at a big pep rally on the grounds.

The 2002 State Fair should have been a Democratic love fest as polls were showing Blagojevich ahead, with Democrats likely to win both the Illinois House and Senate. Instead the first round of an internal party squabble was a harbinger of what came to be the trademark of the Blagojevich years.

Candidate Blagojevich fired the first shot early in the week, telling reporters that Madigan was "arrogant" for steering $1.6 million in state funds to a friend who ran a private livestock show every spring at the fairgrounds. And this at a time of enormous state budget deficits in Illinois. Speaker Madigan was not used to having his authority questioned, especially not by someone from his own party, candidate for governor or not. Traditionally Madigan rarely gives interviews or makes himself available to the press. But this time he acted quickly. He denied that he was arrogant—but conceded that he *was* in a powerful position "where I could be arrogant if I want to be." To further put Blagojevich in his place and let him know early on what it would be like to tangle with the speaker of the House, Madigan said, "I don't plan to be critical of other Democrats. I don't plan to be critical of Blagojevich. I could talk about some of his indiscretions, but I don't plan to do that—because I plan to be a strong party chair and work to bring all Democrats together." Reporters clustered around Madigan—what did he mean by "indiscretions"? Madigan never answered. The warning was enough.

The exchange infuriated Dick Mell. With the rumor mill churning that perhaps "indiscretions" meant Blagojevich had been having an affair, Mell took to the airwaves to defend his daughter, denying any such thing, saying that Patti would not stand for such behavior from her husband. "Knowing Rod Blagojevich and knowing what he thinks of my daughter, I guarantee there are no indiscretions," said Mell. "He'd have it from my daughter. Patti is a very strong-willed young lady." Blagojevich too shot back, declaring that he had no idea what Madigan was talking about—and then went out of his way to emphasize that he would not back down on his criticism of the party chairman. Candidate Blagojevich said, "How could you possibly justify spending money on [a livestock exposition] when you cut funding for health care, when you cut funding for public protection, correctional officers, when you cut funding for mental health facilities?"

This nasty exchange—even before Blagojevich assumed the office of governor—laid the groundwork for a dysfunctional relationship that prevailed between the two powerful political leaders throughout the entire Blagojevich administration.

The new governor's attitude toward the nitty-gritty of the legislative process didn't help matters. In charting a strategy that would help with his ambition to be president, Blagojevich had little interest in the workaday effort that goes into crafting legislation. He preferred to spend his time—and his political capital—in announcing innovative new proposals that would play well on the national stage: universal health care, preschool for all children, equal pay for women. His critics often accused him of governing by press conference, paying little attention to what was necessary to effect the programs he announced.

Mike Madigan was just the opposite kind of officeholder. Madigan loved the details of putting a bill together and was a master of the politics it took to get his legislation passed. He avoided the limelight, preferring to wield his considerable power behind the scenes. A man of precise habits, when in Springfield Madigan ate at the same restaurant nearly every day, rarely drank anything stronger than a diet soda, and was in bed most evenings by ten o'clock.

Charles Wheeler, longtime political reporter and journalism professor, suggests that Mike Madigan is respected by members of the Illinois House because he takes care of them. "The thing that makes Madigan able to exert the influence over his members that he does, is that he is very rarely wrong in his political judgment," Wheeler says. "And his members respect him for that. And he's also someone who is very, very concerned about their welfare in the sense of making sure they can create the kind of record that helps get them reelected."

Critics of Madigan complain that he uses his power ruthlessly. One former legislator has described Madigan's method of working with the legislature: "In Madigan's world, he will come up to a legislator and ask the legislator once for a vote, and the legislator knows he has maybe thirty seconds to make up his mind or Madigan will walk away—and Madigan then will find some way to get his vote. But the legislator will have a black mark on his career for the rest of his tenure."

While the new Blagojevich administration had made promises to reform the state's hiring and firing practices, to many in Springfield its actions looked a lot like old-line political patronage politics—but at a higher price. U.S. Attorney Patrick Fitzgerald began looking into the governor's hiring practices early on, when reports surfaced about a mysterious $1,500 check from Blagojevich's boyhood friend, Michael Ascaridis, that had made its way into the governor's campaign coffers at just about the time Ascaridis's wife received a state job. Blagojevich claimed the $1,500 check was a birthday gift to his daughter Amy.

Blagojevich created another big problem for himself by firing state employees who had worked in the previous Republican administration, even though they were protected from political firings by a 1990 court decision. A 2004 report from the Illinois inspector general's office found that the administration's hiring decisions were even more egregious. The governor's office was controlling hiring, not the various department heads. In other words, illegal patronage hiring and firing was alive and well in the Blagojevich administration.

In the first years Joe Cini was director of the Governor's Office of Intergovernmental Affairs (GOIA), which meant he was Blagojevich's patronage chief and held sway over who would and would not be hired in the Blagojevich administration. The inspector general found that at least 360 people had been awarded their jobs after their applications were sent through back channels by the governor's office or sent in by politically connected officials. That, said Inspector General Zaldwaynaka Scott, showed "not merely an ignorance of the laws, but complete and utter contempt for the law." Four years later, Scott's report was the basis for one of the points in the Article of Impeachment the Illinois House sent to the State Senate.

While many of the battles over hiring and firing were private affairs, the other major struggle in Blagojevich's first term couldn't have been more public. In Illinois from January to June, the General Assembly meets under an obligation to draw up a state budget. Each year it is the most significant item on the legislature's agenda. The Blagojevich administration faced a $5 billion budget shortfall the first year. The governor got around that problem with a massive and controversial borrowing plan that would pile money into the state's five employee pension plans, whose underfunding was responsible for a large portion of the deficit. These were the very same pension plans that Tony Rezko and Stuart Levine were violating to enrich themselves and, according to court testimony, to funnel money into the governor's campaign coffers. The borrowing plan worked this way. Up to $10 billion in bonds would be sold and the money placed in the pension funds, where it would be invested. Legislators balked but finally approved the plan. The budget process hadn't gone as smoothly as legislators had hoped, but at least they believed the budget negotiations for the next fiscal year were complete.

But state government in the Blagojevich era usually ran contrary to conventional wisdom. In a move that initially puzzled, then angered legislators, after the budget had been agreed on Blagojevich called in the state's constitutionally elected officials—the lieutenant governor, attorney general, secretary of state, comptroller, and treasurer—and told them to cut their budgets. He insisted that the cuts were necessary to achieve a balanced budget. It was a move that particularly infuriated Secretary of State Jesse White, who at the time was the leading African-American vote-getter in Illinois. White was in his second term as secretary of state and an extremely popular politician. He was much loved as the founder of the Jesse White Tumbling Team, which gave Chicago's inner-city kids an alternative to guns, gangs, and drugs, and a chance to perform around the country. White, a tumbler himself, is a proud man who, in his sixties, still maintains his athletic physique.

White was appalled by the way Blagojevich handled his first state budget process. He recalls, "The governor called all the constitutional officers up to his office—and as we walked in, he said, 'I didn't want to meet with you but one of my aides insists upon—or thought it was a good idea for me to talk with you personally.' I said, 'Well, whoever that aide was, he should be rewarded because I think it's only fitting and proper that if you are going to have a meeting with us where you're going to cut our budget, I think it would be nice for you to talk with us face to face, and to invite us up to your office in order to do so.' So he said, 'Well, you're here because I need money for the rainy day fund and I need to take from each of the constitutional officers—seven and a half percent.' And I said to him, since I was probably the senior member there, I said, 'Governor, if you take more than three percent from my budget, I'll have to close facilities, lay people off, fire people.' And he said, 'Jesse, that doesn't sound like such a bad idea.'"

White says he was furious for good reason. First, he had just read that Blagojevich had brought in $880,000 from the Service Employees International Union for his campaign fund. Now the governor was sticking it to those union members whose state jobs might be in jeopardy if the budget cut he was asking for was approved.

Second, White pointed out that several weeks later Blagojevich told a school audience that he wanted to put *more* money into the schools, but because Secretary of State Jesse White and others were resisting budget cuts, he couldn't give them the money. Those comments from the governor, White said, made him wonder: what happened to that rainy day fund the governor had talked about in his office?

Ultimately the state's constitutional officers met again with the governor to try to work something out. White said they thought they had a deal. He remembers, "We went to his office and I said to him, 'Governor, the best I can do is to give you three percent, like I said yesterday.' Lisa Madigan said, 'Governor, the same here—three percent.' Judy Baar Topinka [the state treasurer] said, 'Three percent.' And Dan Hines [the comptroller] is on the speaker-phone and [the governor] says, 'Dan, it looks like we have a consensus—it's going to be three percent across the board.' We shook hands and we left."

But it wasn't over yet, White continued. "A couple hours later he called me, called downstairs to my office and said, 'I'd like to amend the three percent—to make it five percent.' I said, 'Governor, we have an agreement at three percent.' He says, 'I'm gonna have a press conference at two o'clock, and I'm gonna announce that I'm taking seven and a half percent!'" White was astonished.

The governor continued his attack on the budget process, calling legislators who opposed his cuts "a bunch of drunken sailors." Finally, the governor used his line-item veto power to cut the budgets of all the constitutional officers, including Jesse White, by seven and a half percent.

White tried to remedy what he regarded as a financial catastrophe by going back to the legislature to try to void some of the governor's actions. He succeeded in collecting enough votes to restore most of the money with one bill. Just as the legislature was on the verge of calling up a second bill that would restore the remainder of the cuts, Blagojevich summoned White to his office. He told him that if he would delay calling up the second bill, the governor would have a press conference and restore the cuts himself.

That wasn't good enough for Jesse White. Standing in the governor's office, toe to toe with Blagojevich, White fumed, "Governor, for whatever you think of [former governor] George Ryan . . . I've known him for thirty years. He never lied to me once. You've lied to me fifteen times in six months."

Six years later, after the governor was arrested by the FBI and accused of trying to sell Obama's U.S. Senate seat, Blagojevich eventually named former state comptroller Roland Burris to fill the seat. It was Secretary of State Jesse White who refused to certify the governor's signature on the certificate of appointment. His action ensnarled the process for several days. Jesse White is a man who does not forget.

That first legislative session in 2003 set the tone for Blagojevich's relationship with the legislature for the ensuing six years. The governor's determination to stick to his campaign promise—not to raise the state income tax or sales tax—made each year's budget process increasingly difficult and contentious. Meanwhile the state's budget deficit continued to grow. Yet the governor's insistence on maintaining his "no tax increase" pledge won him support among Illinois voters. At the end of his first year in office he had a 65 percent approval rating.

His relationship with state representatives and state senators, however, never improved. So little trust existed between the governor and members of the legislature, in fact, that in 2004 lawmakers took the unprecedented step of demanding that the governor sign so-called memoranda of understanding to verify that he would uphold his end of any agreement that was reached. In essence they were saying that the governor's word was no good.

Blagojevich's apparent disdain for the legislators was frequently on painful display, exemplified by his chronic tardiness. A particularly distasteful incident occurred in 2004 when the governor arrived late for the funeral of a popular state senator, Vince Demuzio, who had died at age sixty-two after a long and difficult battle with lung cancer. The lieutenant governor, Pat Quinn, had to step in at the last moment to present the ceremonial state flag, which had been draped on the coffin, to Demuzio's widow. Journalist Charles Wheeler remembered that Mike Madigan was particularly disturbed with the governor's apparent lack of respect. "Madigan found it just this incredibly tasteless thing on the part of the governor—that he wouldn't even go to the cemetery for the funeral of this guy who would have been one of his allies in the Senate. My sense in talking to Madigan was, he was amazed—and just disgusted—at this kind of behavior. . . . It became pretty indicative of Blagojevich's attitude. And over the course of his first few years in office, people began to realize that the guy was all about Rod Blagojevich—and he was not someone who could be trusted."

Some of the harsh feelings against the governor might have been soothed had he spent more time in Springfield, the state capital. But Blagojevich stuck to his promise to Patti that they would raise their girls in their Ravenswood Manor neighborhood in Chicago. His decision not to use the fifty-thousand-square-foot governor's mansion, with its Baccarat crystal chandeliers and a full-time chef, disappointed those who loved to visit and enjoy state functions at the historic site. Even unhappier were ordinary folks, downstate residents who are proud of the beautiful old home.

Legislators were more irked that not only was the first family not in the mansion, the governor was rarely ever in Springfield at all. During legislative sessions Blagojevich would make daily trips from Springfield to Chicago on the state's airplane, at $5,800 per round trip. A former senior adviser to the governor told the House impeachment committee that the press questioned the governor on overuse of the state plane. Blagojevich's response: "Fuck it, fuck them [the press]. It comes with the job." Once in Springfield, the governor rarely interacted with legislators. A top aide admitted to me, "The governor just didn't do what he needed to do, and he did not spend time in Springfield, he did not develop relationships, he did not care enough, he did not respect their work—you know he called them drunken sailors, spending like drunken sailors."

"Even the governor's own cabinet officers usually worked on their own," said Judy Baar Topinka. "I mean, this man didn't *talk* to me. He didn't talk to his *lieutenant governor*, he didn't talk to *any* of his officers. We had no idea what he was doing. The *only* time we ever talked to him was when we got sworn in." According to

Topinka, "Not one cabinet meeting was held during his first term."

To many, Blagojevich was simply an absentee governor. Rarely in Springfield, he could not be found in the governor's office in downtown Chicago either. His absence was a well-kept secret, according to insiders, who also say he left much of the day-to-day decision making to his top aide, Deputy Governor Bradley Tusk. One confides, "As a manager he had very little interest in managing. What you hear about Bradley being the hands-on manager, you know, at whatever age he was—twenty-seven, twenty-eight years old running state government—I mean, that was true." Tusk led senior staff meetings every morning, but the governor never showed up. He rarely sat through policy briefings, asking Tusk to gather the information for him. When staff or policy briefers did manage to see the governor, they were often cursed out with a string of profanity. "Having to deal with the policy wonks was something that he dreaded, and Bradley quickly took us out. You know, Bradley for the most part would communicate the policy stuff to the governor or just make decisions himself," says a former senior aide.

Some of his top staff claim that Blagojevich's reluctance to deal with policy questions or accept more speaking engagements stemmed from a basic lack of confidence. "I think that's fair to say, and you know he just—I mean I hate to sound cliché, but he had a kind of inferiority complex about, you know, sounding dumb, though he's not a dumb guy. . . . He wouldn't want to be challenged on stuff, or you'd brief him on some stuff and it would have some level of detail and he'd get very frustrated very quickly. But it's so weird that he didn't want to go to meetings and didn't want to call people—but when he did go to those meetings, or if he did appear before groups, he did a great job."

As the pressures on him began to mount, Blagojevich retreated to his neighborhood campaign office and to his northwest side home. According to a top aide, he became so isolated by his second term that most of the communication with his senior staff was done by speakerphone from his home. When the Illinois House brought a thirteen-piont article of impeachment against Rod Blagojevich, he could only put on a media blitz looking for popular support. He had none in the Illinois legislature.

10

Flesh and Blood

WHILE THE GOVERNOR was battling the legislature, his relationship with his father-in-law—and the Thirty-third Ward Democratic party in Chicago—was also falling apart. Dick Mell had been delighted to have a son-in-law as governor. But it was not long after Blagojevich assumed office that Mell realized he was being shut out of dealings with the governor's office. Blagojevich and those closest to him, fund-raisers Tony Rezko and Chris Kelly, his chief of staff Lon Monk, and his former legislative aide from Congress John Wyma, all felt that Mell was a liability as they positioned Blagojevich in his governorship and viewed a possible run for president. Dick Mell was old school, with an organization that thrived on loyalty—and patronage. It was not the image Blagojevich wanted as he touted his goals for a reform administration.

Those around Mell say he wasn't interested in benefiting *personally* from Blagojevich's position as governor, as Rezko and Levine were, but he had hoped for some state jobs for the political workers in his ward. And he wanted to be a part of the governor's "kitchen cabinet." At least he wanted the governor's ear. After all, without Dick Mell there never would have been a Governor Rod Blagojevich. It wasn't that Mell wanted to run things—or maybe he did—but he would have been satisfied just to be *in the game*. And he knew that those in his ward organization, who had worked so hard for Blagojevich from the time he had first run for state representative, thought it was time for a little payback. A top precinct captain in Mell's organization, a guy whom Mell had supported for public office, put it this way: "You understand that the Thirty-third Ward—this was their moment to shine. This was the blue-collar ward that had made a governor. They worked hard and put up signs and they went downstate and raised money . . . but already at this time, Chris Kelly had said, 'I'm going to be Rod Blagojevich's Tim Degnan [former patronage chief for Mayor Richard M. Daley].' And he started cutting people out. The first person he was going to cut out was Dick Mell, because he felt Dick Mell represented how they *couldn't* get to the presidency. . . . And even a couple years ago Dick Mell said, 'You know I'm just the kind of guy, if we made up, I would be in Iowa the next day,'" the precinct captain said. "I told him, 'You're fucking nuts.'"

What especially angered the precinct captain is that he saw jobs being passed out by the new administration but *none* of them were coming to the Thirty-third Ward. "Rod likes money people," he said. "It didn't matter how many signs I put up in 2002, didn't matter I was up all night putting up his signs, didn't matter that we were cutting deals or taking out ads or dropping literature. What mattered is how much money you gave. So unlike, let's say, Richard J. Daley or some other guys—or even like the Nineteenth Warders who respect guys who are doing political work, or Mike Madigan—these people are just about money." From his perspective, the precinct captain had painted a pretty accurate picture of what made the Blagojevich administration tick.

Incidents that appeared trivial continued to rankle Mell and his organization. The office staff at the Thirty-third Ward left Blagojevich's name on the ward stationery after he won the election. They were proud of their association with the new governor. Blagojevich did not see it that way. He told his legal counsel to draft a letter to the Thirty-third Ward saying it was illegal to list the governor on their letterhead, and to remove his name. Mell was stunned and unhappy. Chris Kelly summoned Mell to a meeting at a popular downtown health club and laid down some new rules. Kelly told him, "The governor is really mad about this."

"This is my own son-in-law," said Mell. "Rod could have just picked up the phone. We would have taken his name off. It was just goofy!" But that was just the beginning. It grew goofier—and nastier—at a family get-together over Christmas weekend in 2004.

Christmas had always been a special time for the Mell family. Despite rocky relations between her father and her husband, Patti Blagojevich was looking forward to Christmas Eve with her daughters and her family. But sometime during the evening, Rod overheard a conversation about Frankie Schmidt, a distant cousin of Mell's wife, Marge. Schmidt had opened a landfill in Joliet with Mell's help, and supposedly had dropped Blagojevich's name, telling waste haulers that he had clout with the governor and with Mell, and not to worry—the haulers could dump illegal waste without a problem from regulators. Governor Blagojevich didn't say a word about the conversation that night. But several days later he ordered the Illinois Environmental Protection Agency to shut down Schmidt's Joliet landfill.

Mell had already left for his Florida vacation home with his wife when he got the news. He was absolutely livid. He contends to this day that nothing illegal was going on, that he had told Schmidt that he had to be purer than Caesar's wife because of the relationship to Blagojevich. Mell claimed that Frankie Schmidt had implemented the newest scientific technologies, used by few other landfills. He wanted to be certain that the facility received no illegal material. And Mell swore he had no financial involvement in the landfill, saying he had acted only as an adviser to Schmidt. After the Illinois EPA investigated, they agreed that Schmidt was operating honestly, and the landfill was reopened.

But for Mell, when his son-in-law, governor of the State of Illinois, ordered that landfill closed, it sounded the final note in their relationship. What had been building over the past two years in the family exploded in a very public way into Illinois' First Family Feud.

Mell was so angry he couldn't control his emotions. Without considering the damage it would cause his daughter's family, he blasted Governor Blagojevich in a newspaper interview with Fran Spielman of the *Chicago Sun-Times*. Mell accused Blagojevich of ripping apart his family. The governor, he said, was so politically manipulative that he would "throw anyone under the bus. . . . He uses people, and he used me. He uses everybody, and when there's no more use, he discards them." Dick Mell had been humiliated, and he was enraged. Now he wanted revenge.

But Rod Blagojevich wasn't just Dick Mell's son-in-law anymore. He was the governor of Illinois, the highest elected Democrat in the state. The boss. And he fought back. He told reporters, "I have a responsibility as the governor of Illinois to protect the public interest, the public health, the environment, and in this particular case, that responsibility came up against the interest of a member of my family, and when I chose the public, he got mad." He was still repeating that explanation years later, though it never flew with Mell.

Most painful for Mell and his wife was that their daughter was caught in the middle, having to choose between her husband and her father. After the landfill controversy, Patti Blagojevich stopped speaking to her father. For two years there was no contact; the Blagojeviches would not even pick up the phone when Mell called. He lost touch with his two granddaughters, Amy and Anne, whom he adored. One of Mell's greatest joys was taking the two little girls to his vacation home in Lake Geneva, Wisconsin. Now all that was gone. "It's like putting a stake through my heart," Mell told the *Sun-Times*.

Mell didn't hold back his feelings about being shut out of his son-in-law's administration by political newcomers like Chris Kelly. Mell compared himself to an older woman who gets dumped for a trophy wife. He told the reporter, "It's like the case of the individual who marries his childhood sweetheart [who] . . . helped him get through law school or med school or become an actor. Fast-forward twenty years, now he's at the top of his profession. He's a famous doctor. He's the president of the bar association. He gets nominated for an Academy Award. He and the wife now come home from the event, and he says, 'What a great man I am.' And she says, 'Wait a second, I remember you when you were crying that we needed more money or you were crying that you thought you'd fail one of those tests.' He, with his gigantic ego, cannot stand that anymore, so he jettisons that wife and gets a new trophy wife. I am the old wife. The new wife is Chris Kelly."

If Dick Mell had stopped at that, his family relationships might have been salvaged. But he took the next step and went public with an accusation that hammered the first nail in the coffin of the Blagojevich administration. "Christopher Kelly," Mell said, "trades appointments to commissions for checks for $50,000" to the governor's political fund.

Now it was Blagojevich's turn to be livid. At a press conference he told reporters he had the "testicular virility" to stand up to his father-in-law, and demanded that Mell drop the accusations against Kelly. Meanwhile Kelly himself hired a high-powered lawyer and threatened to sue Mell for defamation of character. Two weeks later Mell backed down and apologized, but he couldn't unscramble the egg, and the charges stuck. Illinois attorney general Lisa Madigan opened an investigation that eventually morphed into Patrick Fitzgerald's Operation Board Games. Mell had set in motion the process that would ultimately lead to his son-in-law's arrest.

It was a brutally difficult time for Mell. Not only had he been dropped from the lives of his daughter and granddaughters, but Marge, his wife of forty-two years, had fallen ill with a mysterious and debilitating illness.

It was eventually diagnosed as progressive supranuclear palsy, a disease that ravaged her brain cells. Marge Mell was a beautiful and vibrant woman who had taken over much of the operation of the family's spring manufacturing company so that her husband could indulge his passion for politics. Now Mell was devastated by his wife's illness, and the couple traveled the globe seeking a cure. They had high hopes for experimental stem-cell treatments used by physicians in South Korea and Italy, but the techniques did little to halt Marge Mell's rapid brain deterioration.

Mell's heart was torn apart as he watched the woman he loved lose her ability to walk, speak, or care for herself. "I've spent my life trying to help everybody, and I can't help her," Mell told friends. By nature he was outgoing and gregarious, but he became more and more reclusive as he searched obsessively for a cure. Friends worried about Marge, but they soon became concerned about her husband. As she suffered, he turned to shots of scotch to get him through the long nights.

Guilt plagued Mell too. He remembered his wife's warnings about their son-in-law. She was a good judge of character, and Mell had always respected her opinions about people. She had thought it wasn't the best idea to support Rod for Congress and then for governor. She was concerned, she told her husband, about the trustworthiness of their son-in-law. But Mell had acquiesced to the pleadings of his daughter and to his own desire to be a part of the glorious victories he was certain lay ahead for the young man. Sadly, Mell thought, Marge's instincts had been right on target. The victories had come, but the price was too high to pay.

It wasn't supposed to be this way. This should have been a wonderful time for the Mells, with enough money for a comfortable retirement and homes in Chicago and Florida. Their son-in-law, whom Mell had groomed, had risen to become governor, and they had three beautiful and healthy grandchildren to enjoy. Instead the family was splintered and his wife was dying.

Patti Blagojevich came regularly to visit her mother, but she had very little communication with her father. Rod Blagojevich never visited his terminally ill mother-in-law. On December 3, 2006, Margaret Mell lost her battle with brain disease. She was only sixty-two years old. The day was colder and sadder than anyone could have imagined when Patti and Rod Blagojevich attended her funeral.

Marge's death brought a slight thaw to the relation-ship between Mell and his daughter. But in no sense was the relationship repaired. It was only the arrest of Rod Blagojevich that brought father and daughter back to-gether. Patti Blagojevich had nowhere else to turn except to her family on the day her husband was taken out of their home, handcuffed and in the custody of FBI agents.

Patti Blagojevich feared not only what might happen to her husband but to herself as well, and to her family. As a licensed real estate broker, Patti Blagojevich's real estate dealings caught the eye of federal investigators dur-ing her husband's first term, when it was revealed that one-quarter of her real estate commissions came from deals with her husband's chief fund-raiser, Tony Rezko, who was already under investigation for his dealings with the administration. In December 2007 the *Chicago Tribune* reported that Patti Blagojevich had made more than $700,000 in commissions after her husband began raising money in 2000 for his first run for governor. Of those commissions, more than three-quarters came from real estate deals with political supporters, fund-raisers, and state contractors. In one deal Mark Wight, the head of an architecture and engineering firm, sold his condo to Rod Blagojevich confidant and lobbyist John Wyma for $650,000. Patti Blagojevich received a commission on the sale, and shortly thereafter Wight won $10 million in no-bid state contracts. The governor's office insisted there was no connection between Patti Blagojevich's real estate deals and state contracts. In another instance John H. Simpson, an investment banker who had donated $97,000 to Governor Blagojevich's campaign fund, added Patti Blagojevich as a co-listing agent along with his original agent when he sold his home, netting Blagojevich $32,000 in commissions. "I figured the seller wanted to throw her a little business" said the original agent, Mary Bennett.

Patti Blagojevich was also heard on the FBI wiretaps that dealt with the "selling" of Barack Obama's Senate seat. She suggested she would be qualified to sit on a corporate board, one of the tradeoffs the governor had talked about in exchange for naming a new senator. She was also heard in the background on another tape urging her husband to hold up state funds to help finance a sale of the Chicago Cubs by the *Chicago Tribune* unless *Tribune* editorial board members were fired. She tells her husband, ". . . hold up that fucking Cubs shit . . . fuck them."

After learning that his daughter too had been caught on tape, Mell grew still more concerned about the future of Patti and his granddaughters, though he was enormously relieved that Patti was talking to him again and bringing the girls to the Mell house. But there was no communication with Mell's son-in-law and no softening in that relationship. They say Mell understood the legal boundaries of politics and patronage more clearly than his son-in-law. And by turning away from his father-in-law and looking to Tony Rezko and Chris Kelly for counsel, Rod Blagojevich set foot on a path that led to tragedy for himself, his family, and for the people of the state he had been elected to govern.

Maybe Elvis said it best. Fools rush in where angels fear to tread.

11

Out in Front on Health Care

"I HAVE A DAUGHTER who required what turned out to be three months of inpatient psychiatric care—intensive—which is incredibly difficult for our family, unbelievably difficult, and almost certainly would have forced us to sell our home were it not for the All Kids program. So as far as I'm concerned, he genuinely saved the life of my child, and I say this: I give him credit for it, because I don't really follow Springfield politics that closely. But even before it affected me personally I knew that this is the one thing this guy is really obsessed with."

Health care, and particularly children's health care, was Rod Blagojevich's signature issue. His public commitment to it brought him passionate support from many people in Illinois, like this father whose daughter had three months of inpatient psychiatric care paid for by the Illinois All Kids initiative.

As debates over adequate health care raged across the country, Governor Rod Blagojevich pushed Illinois onto center stage by making it the first state in the nation to offer universal health-care coverage for children. The vehicle was called the All Kids program, and provided coverage for all Illinois children whose families could not afford private insurance.

While most legislators agreed with the governor in wanting to expand access to health care, debates over how it should be done were tumultuous and angry. When Blagojevich was unable to get what he wanted from the House and Senate, he often performed an end run around the legislature, using his powers as governor to launch new programs. As popular as his major health initiatives were with the citizens of Illinois, three of those initiatives became the seeds of charges at the governor's impeachment trial. Legislators accused Blagojevich of abuse of power when he acted to expand access to health care.

The first of these actions occurred in October 2004, when a flu epidemic swept the country and the U.S. Food and Drug Administration warned of a shortage of flu vaccine. As unbelievable as it seemed, half the nation's entire stock of flu vaccine had been ordered from a single factory in England. If that wasn't risky enough, the factory's license to manufacture the vaccine had been suspended by the United Kingdom because of contamination of the serum. That left the United States with a severe shortage of flu vaccine during a massive flu outbreak. Health officials asked only those most at risk—the elderly, infants, pregnant women, health-care workers—to get a flu shot.

For Blagojevich it was a tailor-made issue. If he could somehow bring more vaccine into the country, he could provide a real service for people—and gain some impressive national headlines. He soon had his administration jumping through hoops. Within four days of the FDA's announcement of the shortage, the governor's people were using their contacts (built up in another controversial program to allow seniors to import drugs from Canada) to find a drug company abroad that could manufacture the flu vaccine for use in the United States.

In his fiery speech at his impeachment trial the about-to-be-ex-governor defended his actions at the time: "I was foreseeing the possibility that elderly and infants might be vulnerable to flus that could conceivably take their lives. To me it was a no-brainer. Get the flu vaccine."

The governor's special advocate for prescription drugs arranged a tentative contract with the British firm of Ecosse Hospital Products for the delivery of 35,000 doses of vaccine. Then the order was raised to 300,000 doses to ensure an adequate supply for Illinois' priority population. The cost was $2.6 million. Governors from five other states—New York, Tennessee, New Mexico, Kansas, and Ohio—watching Blagojevich's initiatives, asked Illinois to procure vaccine for their states as well, which brought the total cost to $8.2 million. But there was a big hitch: the FDA refused to approve the importation of the European vaccine.

In December the Centers for Disease Control announced that it had located enough flu vaccine for Illinois' priority population. Despite the CDC's announcement, the Blagojevich administration went ahead with the purchase of the vaccine and continued to urge the FDA to allow the European vaccine into the country. "We have been working with the FDA for more than two months to give them all the relevant information about the vaccine from Europe they need to approve our request. . . . They've dragged their feet on the Illinois request. The risk is far too great for them to continue this waiting game," Blagojevich pleaded. But the FDA approval never came through, and not a single dose of vaccine was ever delivered to Illinois or any other state. The vaccine Illinois had acquired was finally donated to the nation of Pakistan, but it had to be destroyed because it had expired by the time it arrived.

The question, then, was: who would pay for the $8.2 million of vaccine that was never delivered? At first Ecosse attempted to get Illinois to pay for the entire amount, but then the company backed off and filed a suit for $2.6 million.

Was the entire fiasco an impeachable offense? The House impeachment committee said it was, because the governor knew the CDC would find enough vaccine and would not approve the European vaccine. Therefore when he went ahead and purchased the vaccine, Blagojevich had entered into a contract that violated state and federal laws.

Speaking before the Illinois Senate at his impeachment trial, Blagojevich pointed out that the state had not lost money on the flu vaccine deal, that the matter was still in court. "I pursued what I believe was the moral and right thing to do," he said, "with the legal means to do them, helping families make sure they had the flu vaccines that are necessary to keep them alive."

At the same time Blagojevich was attempting to bring in European flu vaccine, he was in the midst of another high-profile health-care issue—making low-cost Canadian prescription drugs available for citizens of Illinois. At the time, American senior citizens had begun chartering buses to Canada to buy prescription drugs at much cheaper cost than in the United States. The issue had grown into something of a political bombshell. Despite staunch opposition from the Bush administration and a cry of outrage from the U.S. pharmaceutical industry, bills were being introduced in Congress that would allow the importation of lower-priced drugs from Canada.

In January 2009, speaking in his own defense at his impeachment trial, Blagojevich told the state senators how he first got involved. "The idea came to me not from me, but from then-Congressman Rahm Emanuel—my congressman. He came to me with a good idea and said, 'Why don't you lead the charge and lead the fight on this and be the first state to go to Canada and test whether or not the FDA will allow you to do it or not? Think about the morality of this. Think about how we can help our seniors. And think about what we can do to help families.' And I loved the idea—and we did it. And then, so did Wisconsin and so did Kansas and so did Vermont."

Again it was a perfect vehicle for Blagojevich—a big bold move, a chance to help people as well as grab national attention. It was just the right issue for someone looking to mount a campaign for president.

In September 2003 Blagojevich, with the help of Congressman Emanuel, asked the FDA to reverse the policy that prohibited state and local governments from importing drugs from Canada, where prices were 30 to 50 percent lower. While it was not illegal for individuals or private health-care plans to bring in prescription drugs from Canada, the FDA barred states and local governments from doing so. The Blagojevich administration estimated that the state could save $91 million by allowing state employees covered under Illinois state insurance plans to buy their prescription drugs from Canada. Governors in other cash-strapped states joined Illinois in a national media and lobbying campaign aimed at pressuring the FDA to change its rules. Congressman Emanuel's bill, which allowed prescription drugs to be imported from Canada, passed in the House, but it stalled in the Senate and never became law.

Nearly a year after the plan was announced, and still without FDA approval, Blagojevich launched the "I-Save-Rx" program, which gave Illinois consumers access to prescription drugs from Canada. The governor declared, "We have taken every possible step we could think of to convince the FDA, the Congress, and anyone and everyone who will listen, that people across Illinois, and across our country, deserve access to safe and lower-cost prescription drugs. . . . We can't keep asking people to spend more money than they have—just to afford the medicine they need." The governor's announcement promised numerous safety measures to ensure the quality and safety of the drugs, including state inspections of the pharmacies and wholesalers distributing them.

Blagojevich continued to tout the I-Save-Rx program as one of his administration's finest achievements. But ultimately the Illinois House committee on impeachment saw it quite differently. The committee concluded that, because Illinois' drug importation program had never received the approval of the FDA, Blagojevich had again violated state and federal law. The committee believed the governor's promised state inspections of foreign pharmacies were inadequate, and the state had never tested prescription drugs received under the program. "In sum," the impeachment committee concluded, "the Governor knew the program was illegal but allowed it to go forward; and then the program, once implemented, violated numerous State laws relating to safety and quality control of prescription drugs." Committee members noted that they did not oppose the attempt to help individuals save on the cost of prescription drugs. But because the governor's program was illegal, he had abused the power of his office, and that, they said, was an impeachable offense.

But the biggest battle between Blagojevich and the legislature was not over the importation of flu vaccine or prescription drugs. It concerned the expansion of access to health insurance for children and families. This fight too mirrored the larger debate going on across the country about reform of the largely broken American health-care system. With the support of the Illinois legislature, and with funding from the federal government, under the Blagojevich administration 400,000 more children were given access to health care. But the Blagojevich dream—to become one of the first states in the union to provide universal health care for all—eventually lay in ashes, destroyed by bitter political infighting and a battered economy. The proposed expansion also became the gist of a point in the article of impeachment brought against the governor in 2008.

Blagojevich's campaign to provide universal health care in Illinois began seriously in 2004 with the passage of the Health Care Justice Act. This measure set a goal of developing a plan for universal coverage by July 1, 2007. It also established the Adequate Health Care Task Force, with members appointed by the General Assembly and the governor, and including representatives from physician groups, hospital administrators, insurance companies, state agencies, and lawmakers. The task force met for three years, held public hearings in every Illinois congressional district, and in January 2007 issued its final report calling for near-universal coverage while retaining an employer-based system.

Shortly after the release of this final report, the governor announced "Illinois Covered," his plan to provide universal coverage in Illinois. It promised coverage for 1.4 million uninsured adults in Illinois at a price tag of $2.1 billion. The plan contained many of the same elements developed by the Health Care Task Force. But Jim Duffett, executive director of the Campaign for Better Health Care, the advocacy group that helped create the task force, says the governor made a strategic mistake by not taking advantage of the support built up for universal health care by the task force's years of work: "We wish that there would have been more of an attempt by the governor to reach out to House and Senate members and build at least a broader coalition in pushing his proposal. Instead he just initially did this on his own, and I think that was, you know, a mistake."

Illinois Covered also got caught up in the ongoing, bruising political battle between Governor Blagojevich and House Speaker Michael Madigan. In that conflict Blagojevich did have in his corner Emil Jones, president of the Senate. Jones, a stocky African American with a distinctive, deep gravel voice, had taken over the reins as Senate president at age sixty-eight after thirty years in the Illinois legislature. It was the crowning achievement in the career of a man who had grown up impoverished on Chicago's South Side. Jones had been raised in a family of eight children. His father was a stern, hardworking truck driver, who was also a Democratic precinct captain.

Jones came from the old school of politics. He understood the art of the deal and was a master at successfully moving along legislation that fit his agenda of helping the poor and disadvantaged. He was also a shrewd judge of talent. Barack Obama called him his political godfather after Jones took the young state senator under his wing and sent legislation his way that would boost his political reputation.

Emil Jones became president of the Senate as a result of the same election that sent Rod Blagojevich to the governor's office. Republicans were crushed by the weight of the George Ryan scandals. Jones looked at the election results as an opportunity to pass legislation long blocked by Republicans—items such as health-care reform and funding for education—which were also at the top of the Blagojevich agenda. Those issues, Jones maintains, were at the root of his continued support for the increasingly embattled governor.

Jones recalled, "I stuck with him based on certain issues. Then the other political reason I stuck with the governor was simply because I wanted to see him be successful. We hadn't had a Democratic governor in twenty-five years—so why destroy the governor? I overlooked a lot of things that he did, and I attempted to help him. I wanted him to be successful as a governor." Jones's critics say he stuck with the governor because of the large number of his own family members who were on the state payroll.

The Senate president championed Blagojevich's Illinois Covered when it was introduced in the Senate. The plan survived its first test in early May 2007 when the Senate Public Health Committee approved it. Blagojevich pronounced it a major victory: "Across Illinois, families are struggling to pay health-care costs—or forgoing medical care entirely—because they don't have access to affordable health care. That isn't right. Today's committee vote is a good first step toward giving middle-class families real access to affordable health-care insurance."

At the same time Blagojevich was pushing his universal health-care plan, he was locked in the biggest budget battle of his five years in office. As a candidate for governor, Blagojevich had promised no tax increases. As governor he continued to insist there would be no increase in the state income tax or sales tax. That firm stand stymied legislators in their efforts to find revenues to cover serious budget deficits—and paying for a $2.1 billion universal health-care plan they considered out of the question.

But Governor Blagojevich was adamant: there would be universal health care. And, he said, he had a funding mechanism that would overcome the budget deadlock. He would accept a new tax on the gross receipts of businesses with more than $2 million a year in revenues. The new tax, said the governor, would generate more than $7 billion a year for the state—enough to fund universal health care and educational reform. With his enormous political war chest, Blagojevich launched a two-month blitz of TV ads and personal-appearance rallies attacking those who opposed the gross receipts tax as "fat cats" and "corporate freeloaders." In several speeches he even cast his critics as "sinners."

The populist governor told the citizens of Illinois, "This is more than a fight, this is a crusade. It will be Armageddon, but we are on the side of the Lord."

Even staunch health-care advocates were stunned by this rhetoric. It was a tactic that Blagojevich often used as governor: set up a straw man and lash out, rather than talk about, the idea he was proposing. Business groups, including the Illinois Chamber of Commerce and representatives of the insurance industry, immediately struck back. House Speaker Michael Madigan, who already had Blagojevich on his hit list, saw a golden opportunity to score a major victory in his long-running feud with the governor. Madigan called for a vote on a nonbinding resolution asking House members if they supported the governor's gross receipts tax plan. The result was overwhelming—107 to 0! No one wished to be recorded as a supporter of a tax increase. It was a brilliant move on Madigan's part. Even the governor's floor leader, his old roommate Jay Hoffman, voted against the tax. Blagojevich had put the legislators in a box: they needed to find revenues for the state budget, but they feared to raise taxes in opposition to the governor's "no tax" pledge.

The governor's reaction to the vote was bizarre. Instead of expressing disappointment or anger, he said, "Today, I think, was basically an up—I feel good about it." No one understood what he meant.

When in August the General Assembly finally approved a budget, it did not include funding for expanded health-care coverage. The governor immediately slashed $463 million from it, saying he would use the money he was cutting from pork-barrel projects to support health-care expansion. As negotiations for health coverage continued, the governor's Illinois Covered price tag was pared from $2.1 billion to $1.2 billion, with the program phased in over four years, not two.

Now America's Agenda, a national nonprofit advocacy group that supports universal health care, became involved in the struggle. The group was eager to see a large Midwest state like Illinois pass a comprehensive health-care bill. In a Washington, D.C., press conference sponsored by America's Agenda, former congressman Dick Gephardt and labor leaders from the AFL-CIO and the Service Employees International Union called for support for Governor

Blagojevich's Illinois Covered. Gephardt told reporters, "I know firsthand the strength of pressures against real health-care reform that operate on Capitol Hill, regardless of which party holds the majority. Enactment of a well-designed plan like 'Illinois Covered' will provide a working state template for members of Congress to examine. It will set a bottom line for the kind of national health-care reform Congress ultimately enacts."

Demonstrating his strong commitment, Gephardt made weekly trips to Illinois to meet with both Blagojevich and Madigan to see if a bill could be drafted that both could live with. Blagojevich gradually agreed to changes in Illinois Covered, but Madigan remained unmoved. A small group of House members who supported the legislation were particularly annoyed when Madigan ignored them at a meeting about the health-care legislation, advising them "to do what they wanted to do" before turning back to the work on his desk. It was clear that the speaker would not be supporting the governor's program.

Senate president Emil Jones believed the reasons behind Speaker Madigan's opposition were clear: "The Speaker's bent on breaking the governor . . . starving the government of revenue—when you starve the government of revenue, it doesn't fall back on the lawmakers. It falls on the chief executive officer."

Jones was neither the first nor the only Illinois politician to attribute Madigan's motives to a desire to help his daughter, Illinois attorney general Lisa Madigan, become the state's next governor. Jones observed of Madigan, "He wanted to make him [Blagojevich] look bad so that people would be upset with the governor—then he could bring his daughter in and run for governor. Do you understand? That's what it's all designed to do."

Whether those were indeed Madigan's motives, he succeeded in blocking nearly all legislation to expand health care. Jones and the health-care advocates finally decided they might be able to pass some portions of the plan if they broke the Illinois Covered package into five separate pieces. Their actions met with limited success. They did pass a bill requiring insurance companies to extend health coverage for dependents up to age twenty-six (thirty if the dependent is a veteran) by allowing them to remain on their parents' health insurance policies.

In November 2007 the governor took a giant step to expand health care, making an end run around the legislature by issuing an executive order to enact another portion of Illinois Covered. He increased the income eligibility requirements for the state's Family Care Health Insurance program, from an annual income of $38,000 to almost $83,000 for a family of four. The change added about 147,000 parents and caretakers to the program.

Announcing his order at a Chicago press conference, Blagojevich said, "I'm going to continue to do what I think is right, and that's one of the good things about being governor. You can do things like this."

"No, actually you can't," said opposing lawmakers. In Illinois, as in many states, when new programs are enacted or changes made to existing ones, the legislature's Joint Committee on Administrative Rules (JCAR) must review the provisions before they take effect. Thus in the wake of the governor's order, the Illinois Department of Health and Human Services submitted a request to JCAR for an emergency rules change, asking for coverage to be preserved for forty thousand people with incomes between $29,000 and $38,000, citing a glitch in Bush administration policy, and asking for the additional expansion as well.

When JCAR ruled that the expansion plan was illegal and must be suspended immediately, it didn't slow the Blagojevich administration a bit. They continued to sign up new enrollees at a cost of $43 million a year. The governor declared that JCAR had only an advisory role and could not trump his executive authority.

That action became, in essence, the ninth point in the article of impeachment brought against the governor. It charged him with abusing the power of his office and exceeding his constitutional authority by expanding the option to purchase health-care insurance, knowing JCAR had made that expansion illegal.

Behind the scenes there were disagreements among the impeachment committee members on whether the expansion of health care was an impeachable offense. Several of the members voiced concerns about appearing as though they were opposed to health-care reform. Ultimately, those concerns were trumped by the argument that a significant pattern of abuse of power had been established by the governor.

In his impassioned closing argument at his impeachment trial, Blagojevich challenged the ninth point of the article. He told the assembled senators, "I've been given legal advice by lawyers and I believe they're right—and other courts have agreed that those lawyers were right—that JCAR is an advisory committee, that it cannot dictate to the executive branch, that if the executive branch seeks to do something, that committee can advise you and suggest whether it's right or wrong, or they agree with you—or not. But they can't stop you. . . . Nine states—nine states—have challenged this case. And in all nine states, the right of the executive branch to do what it sought to do, without the consent of JCAR, was upheld."

In the end, one of the governor's priorities—becoming one of the few states in the country to provide universal health-care coverage for the uninsured—was handled with such poor political strategy that it not only resulted in failed policy but became a key reason why Governor Rod Blagojevich was booted out of office as the fortieth governor of Illinois.

12

It's About the Money

AS THE 2006 gubernatorial election approached, Governor Blagojevich spent less and less time out on the campaign trail talking to voters. He had always been energized by campaigning and effective on the stump. Now it was no fun as he was dogged by reporters asking about the scandals in his administration.

Patrick Fitzgerald's investigation, Operation Board Games, was beginning to bear fruit as the November election day neared. On October 11, 2006, Blagojevich insiders Tony Rezko and Stuart Levine were indicted by Fitzgerald. The two Blagojevich fund-raisers were charged with attempting to extort millions from those seeking to do business with the Illinois Health Facilities Planning Board and the Illinois Teachers' Retirement System. Rezko and Levine, the indictment charged, were raising money for "Public Official A"—later identified by a federal court judge as Governor Rod Blagojevich.

When the indictments were announced Blagojevich downplayed the influence of Rezko in his administration.

"If in fact these allegations relating to Tony are true, he betrayed my trust," Blagojevich said. "He lied to me. He deceived me. But a lot more important than that, he violated the public trust."

One week later Stuart Levine pleaded guilty to scheming to squeeze millions from firms seeking to do business with the Health Facilities Planning Board and the TRS. The plea agreement identified Tony Rezko and "Individual B" as the two leading Blagojevich fund-raisers who had aided Levine in his illegal schemes. "Individual B" was later identified as Chris Kelly.

So just two weeks before the vote for Blagojevich's second term, Fitzgerald laid out a clear pattern of corruption in the governor's administration, indicting one of his closest confidants, Tony Rezko, and taking a guilty plea from his co-schemer, Stuart Levine. Governor Blagojevich continued adamantly to deny any knowledge of the corruption that appeared to be engulfing his administration. And for whatever reason the Blagojevich spin worked: Fitzgerald's blockbuster charges made barely a dent in Blagojevich's lead in the polls.

Despite the brewing corruption charges and the deep-seated distrust between House Speaker Michael Madigan and Governor Blagojevich, Madigan had signed on as co-chairman of the Blagojevich for Governor campaign, a fact that was not forgotten when he began pushing to impeach the governor just two years later. Senate President Emil Jones became the other co-chairman. The Blagojevich fund-raising operation continued to bring in unprecedented amounts of campaign cash, enabling him to drown out his opponent's message. Blagojevich had $18 million in his campaign fund even before the Democratic primary in March. Although he faced a credible primary opponent in Edwin Eisendrath, a former Chicago alderman and HUD regional administrator in the Clinton administration, Blagojevich's huge cash advantage in the purchase of media advertising simply overwhelmed Eisendrath. And just as Blagojevich hoped, his war chest kept other potential challengers from even considering a race against him. Eisendrath hammered at corruption in the Blagojevich administration, but he lost with less than 30 percent of the vote.

The fund-raising prowess of the Blagojevich campaign was aided by weak campaign finance laws in Illinois. Unlike federal campaign finance rules, Illinois laws place no restrictions on campaign contributions and allow unlimited donations from any source. Thus soliciting money from contractors who do business with the state is perfectly legal. And since there is no limit on what those state contractors may give, the Blagojevich fund-raisers could go after them with impunity. Contributions of any size from corporations and unions are also legal. The check on corruption in Illinois was supposed to be disclosure—since the public could then easily see connections between those who donate to campaigns and those who get state business. But a national report on state campaign finance laws, released in February 2007, found that the Illinois disclosure laws were easily evaded. Politicians could get around the disclosure laws because the State Board of Elections, which enforced these laws, was evenly divided between Republicans and Democrats. That made board members wary of investigating cases because both political parties might have to play by the rules. So there were rarely any repercussions for evading campaign disclosure requirements. In a state with a rich history of political corruption and weak campaign finance laws, it was all the more likely that "business as usual" would continue in Illinois.

The Campaign for Political Reform eventually found that in the six years Blagojevich was governor, he raised $56 million, more by far than any previous gubernatorial candidate in the state's history. George Ryan, the governor who preceded him, was able to raise a respectable $20 million over six years. But in Ryan's entire thirty-year political career he raised only $40 million—no match for Blagojevich's astonishing six-year record $56 million. The Republican governor who preceded Ryan, Jim Edgar, raised $11 million for his campaign coffers over six years.

In addition to raising so much more money, Blagojevich raised it in much greater chunks. In a story headlined "The Governor's $25,000 Club," the *Chicago Tribune* analyzed campaign disclosure documents and found that 235 donors had each given exactly $25,000 dollars to the Blagojevich campaign since the year 2000. Of those 235 donors, three of every four received something from the state in return—state contracts, board appointments, or favorable action on policy or regulatory issues. In the campaigns of Blagojevich's predecessors, $25,000 checks were rare. Ryan pulled in only fourteen, and Governor Edgar even fewer. A leading Blagojevich fundraiser, Myron Cherry, told the *Tribune* that it wasn't unusual to list $25,000 as the requested amount on fundraising invitations for those who would agree to be co-hosts. Cherry had no problem with that. He gave two $25,000 contributions—and six months later his law firm won $900,000 in state legal business. Cherry denied any connection. All the other $25,000 donors reported there was no connection at all between their contributions and their business with the State of Illinois—though three-fourths of them received millions of dollars in lucrative state contracts. ACS State and Local Solutions, a company that anted up its first $25,000 contribution in Blagojevich's first year in the governor's office, followed with three more contributions that totaled $25,000; ACS received a yearly average of $17 million in state contracts *every year* Blagojevich was in office. Patrick Engineering, which averaged $14 million in state contracts *every year*, contributed more than $56,000 to the Blagojevich campaign fund. A direct quid pro quo between any contributor and the Blagojevich administration was never proven—but the fund-raising pattern could not have been clearer.

According to Cindi Canary from the Campaign for Political Reform, Governor Blagojevich was stingy with his riches. Says Canary, "The governor was very tight with his funds. In between election periods he spent money on pollsters, media services, consultants. But he made no contributions to others. . . . With Rod Blagojevich there was no spreading of the wealth. He was not building a political organization. We see no evidence that he was out there rewarding people for their good political work. It was really a complete quid pro quo—give me the money and I'll give you the position. So it was a very bold transaction where ultimately the resources went to the Blagojevich Fund or to the Blagojeviches."

By the time of the November 2006 election, Blagojevich had amassed $27 million for his campaign. His opponent in that election, former state treasurer Judy Baar Topinka, says running against an opponent with a $27 million fund was like getting hit by a tsunami.

Topinka was an interesting candidate. She had been the state treasurer during Blagojevich's first term—the only Republican holding statewide office during his administration. After a twenty-six-year career in politics, she had set her sights on becoming the first woman governor of Illinois. As a moderate Republican, Topinka had pulled the beleaguered party together as state Republican chairman after the George Ryan corruption scandals—a thankless and awful job. She was at the GOP helm in 2004 when State Senator Barack Obama announced he would run for the vacant U.S. Senate seat in Illinois. Late in the campaign the GOP's main candidate went down in flames after a sex scandal, and Illinois Republicans had to import Alan Keyes from Maryland to run against Obama. Keyes was clobbered by Obama—and Topinka's party was in a mess.

Topinka is an outspoken woman of Czech and Slovak ancestry, with bright red hair and dark eyes. She was a quirky and memorable candidate. Although the sixty-two-year-old Topinka often got herself into hot water for statements that were too blunt, her career was never marred by political scandal. She was a likable and quite funny lady. After a tough Republican primary, Topinka emerged victorious—but broke. She simply could not withstand the Blagojevich fund-raising juggernaut.

Topinka recalls, "If we made $25,000 off an evening, I felt that we had really done well. I was out on the street. I was holding fund-raisers. I'd go to Republican gatherings—any gathering that would have me—to try to bring in money in what I would call the 'normal way' when running for office. He'd have a night at the Field Museum and bring in $4 million. And I'd come back to my campaign crew and ask, 'Why can't we do that? What's the problem?'

Then I realized that many of my supporters were also going to *his* events. And so I asked, 'Why are you going?' And they said, 'Because we're afraid. We have contracts. We have bids out—and he'll just come after us.' So they'd go, and they'd give money—money that normally goes to Republicans. . . . I have a business lobbyist who came into my office—he's always supported me. The man had tears running down his cheeks and said, 'Judy, I'd love to help you. My people love you,' and so on, and 'We've always been together. We agree on issues. But we're just afraid. We can't support you.'"

Topinka managed to raise $11 million, ordinarily more than enough for a governor's race. But it gave her little traction against Blagojevich, especially after he poured millions into campaign commercials that tied her to the scandals of George Ryan.

True to her Czech heritage, Topinka loved to do the polka and was often photographed leading various politicians in a rousing turn around the dance floor. When the Blagojevich campaign found a video of Topinka dancing with George Ryan, they used it in a highly effective political ad.

Topinka remembered, "He had all this money. He didn't have to leave his house—he could sit down and comb his hair and just run those commercials of me dancing with George Ryan. You know what? My polka with George Ryan didn't cost this state anything. My polka with Vice President Cheney never cost this state anything! My polkas with just about everybody who would polka with me never cost this state anything! It was just a dance. And that commercial was played all the time—making me look like George Ryan's love child! It was great advertising. It was great propaganda. He murdered me on that because I could not fight back."

On election night, in spite of the scandals—in spite of the indictments of those close to the governor—Rod Blagojevich won 49 percent of the vote to Topinka's 40 percent. At his victory party, Blagojevich told a cheering crowd at the Finkl Steel plant in Chicago, "I'm all shook up!" Then he set the tone for his second term as governor: "You ain't seen nothing yet! Strap on your seat belts! Put on your helmets! Get ready to roll! We've got a lot more work to do for the people of Illinois!"

As it turned out, Blagojevich himself would need the seat belt and helmet. His second term proved to be even rockier than the first. U.S. Attorney Patrick Fitzgerald kept the pressure on with more indictments from his Operation Board Games investigation—Nicholas Hurtgen, Dr. Robert Weinstein, William Cellini, Ali Chaab. On June 4, 2008, Fitzgerald scored his most important victory yet. Federal jurors carried their verdict back into the courtroom: Tony Rezko guilty on sixteen of the twenty-four counts against him, convicted of political corruption in the Blagojevich administration. Rezko, an American dream of success, on that day went from the federal courtroom straight to jail.

Patrick Fitzgerald's prosecutors held off on a sentencing hearing for Rezko, employing the classic squeeze—leaving Rezko in jail to see if he would talk, in hopes of reducing his prison time. Fitzgerald and his prosecutors believed they were closing in on the biggest player.

Meanwhile there were large changes afoot in the governor's office. Bradley Tusk, the young, tough-talking deputy governor, had finally wearied of the scene in Springfield. He resigned and headed to New York to become Mayor

Michael Bloomberg's campaign manager for his 2009 run for a third term. Following Tusk's departure, John Harris, former budget director for Chicago's Mayor Daley, took over as chief of staff in the governor's office. Joining Harris as senior adviser to Blagojevich was a former investigative television reporter from Chicago, Bob Arya.

Arya says he was taken aback as soon as he began his new job, because he discovered that Governor Blagojevich was rarely in either of his two offices, in Springfield or Chicago. Arya recalls, "During my time as senior adviser, he showed up at the Thompson Center in Chicago [the primary state office building in the city], which he made his home base, maybe a dozen times." Arya would arrive from his suburban home at 5:30 a.m. at the Thompson Center, and meet with John Harris shortly after 7:00. The two men, along with Deputy Governor Sheila Nix, would map out the day's priorities. Harris would then put in a call to Blagojevich at his home.

Throughout the day the senior staff would communicate with the governor via speakerphone from his home. According to Arya, these conversations were often tense. "The Governor's tone and tenure with respect to those interactions was violently unpredictable—depending on the time of day, his mood, and the issue you were calling about," says Arya. "Many staffers cringed at the notion of calling him—and we were under strict orders to never let the phone ring more than three times. . . . In short, if his day was good, you might have a civilized conversation. If it was not, you could count on a peppering of the 'F' word and a host of other terms generally reserved for street-thug use."

Arya remembers that Blagojevich showed little interest in the day-to-day details of governing, leaving most of the decision-making to Harris and Arya. Just as Bradley Tusk had been the de facto governor during the first term, Arya says that Harris and a few other senior staffers were, in effect, running the State of Illinois in the second term. But, says Arya, Harris could not "handle" Blagojevich as Tusk had done. "Rod was such a high-maintenance person that the role of the deputy governor was basically as a baby-sitter for him—try to make Blagojevich feel good and understand that when bad press appeared, it wasn't his fault, it was just the press *against* him. Bradley Tusk could—and I witnessed this several times—put Rod in his place. When Rod would drop the F-bomb, Bradley was the only guy who would stuff it right back in his face," Arya recalls.

Governor Blagojevich's aversion to face-to-face interaction applied not just to his own staff. His absence extended to meetings with the state's other constitutional officers. The newly elected state treasurer, Alexi Giannoulias, assumed he would be sitting down with the governor to map strategy for the state's increasingly desperate budget problems. But, says Giannoulias, he was never, ever called into the governor's office. "It would seem sensible to me if I were the governor, the chief executive, to get people around me who deal with the stuff every day, and who might provide an opinion, or give you their advice, or might have ideas of their own," says an amazed Giannoulias. "He didn't want anyone else around him, and again that's reflective of his leadership style—very confrontational, very 'I don't want to hear other people's opinions,' very 'It's my way or the highway' . . . and 'If you're not with me, you're against me,' and 'I'll destroy you even if you're doing it because you have ideological differences.' I think this created a horrendous environment in Springfield."

Experienced legislators too chafed at the methods of the Blagojevich administration. Julie Hamos, a respected Democratic state legislator from the Chicago area, had worked for years to find a successful funding formula for mass transit in the state. The situation had become so serious that in January 2008 the mass transit system in Chicago, which carries nearly three million passengers every day, was in danger of shutting down completely. Finally Hamos persuaded Blagojevich to attend a meeting on the problem. Says the astonished legislator, "He came to this meeting and was like a kid out of his element—making campaign speeches, sitting at a table. We were trying to reach resolution of some really thorny and important issues, and he'd be making campaign speeches, using populist jargon and running around the room, bouncing off the walls. It was stunning to watch. . . . I don't think he ever took seriously what government, what governing was all about."

What Blagojevich *was* serious about, say those close to him, was running for President of the United States. He had used the prestigious Washington, D.C., communications firm of Squier, Knapp and Dunn for both his campaigns for governor, and for laying out a strategy for a run for the White House. Bob Arya, who wrote many of the governor's speeches, says most speeches had to be vetted through Bill Knapp, Blagojevich's longtime Washington media consultant, with an eye on the governor's national ambitions.

"Knapp had a very strong influence on Rod. I drafted the first budget address that he gave in '07, including the gross receipts tax," Arya recalls. "It had to be faxed to Bill Knapp, who was on his way to the Virgin Islands. He came up with some changes that vilified business—you know, Blagojevich was running a national populist agenda through Bill Knapp! I mean Knapp was determining the state's priorities because he was trying to set Rod up in the national spotlight! So it was all a plan on Knapp's part to try to get Rod maximum national attention."

But Blagojevich watched as his expensive, carefully crafted plans to run for the presidency were brushed aside by the historic—and meteoric—rise of his Illinois Democratic colleague, U.S. Senator Barack Obama. Obama's road to the White House was exactly the one Blagojevich had hoped to travel. Today many political observers say that some of Blagojevich's erratic behavior stems from his deep disappointment at having his plans eclipsed by Obama's success.

Unlike other Illinois politicians, Rod Blagojevich was shut out from benefiting in any way from Obama's rise to national prominence. As the taint from Patrick Fitzgerald's Operation Board Games continued to spread, the Obama camp moved to distance itself from Governor Blagojevich, particularly concerning their mutual ties to Tony Rezko. It was a connection that did tarnish Obama to a small degree during his presidential campaign, when it became known that Obama had purchased a lot adjacent to his Hyde Park home with the assistance of Tony Rezko's wife—the action Obama later called a "boneheaded move."

Rod Blagojevich was the only prominent Illinois politician without a speaking role at the Democratic National Convention in Denver when Obama secured the party's nomination. Blagojevich hadn't wanted to go to the convention at all and had to be pushed into attending by his staff. He disliked large political gatherings unless he was the main attraction; he rarely attended governor's conferences or other large political events. He showed up on the third day of the convention and put in a two-hour appearance on the convention floor to vote for the nomination of Barack Obama for president. His staff wanted him to stay for Obama's acceptance speech the following night, but Blagojevich had had enough. He had hoped to be the one accepting the Democratic nomination for president. While Obama stood before 84,000 cheering supporters packed into the Invesco Field football stadium, a bitterly disappointed Blagojevich was back in Chicago.

On the warm and historic evening of Tuesday, November 4, 2008, as Barack Obama claimed his victory before 700,000 deliriously happy supporters in Chicago's Grant Park, the governor of Illinois had been told he was not welcome. Just one month later, Rod Blagojevich was arrested by the FBI.

13

Senate Seat for Sale

"I'VE GOT this thing and it's fucking golden, and, uh, I'm just not giving it up for fuckin' nothing. I'm not gonna do it."

The day after Barack Obama's November 4 victory rally in Grant Park, Blagojevich was caught on a wiretapped phone, telling a chief adviser that since he had the power to pick a replacement for Obama's Senate seat, he was going to make the most of it. To the FBI agents listening in—and to U.S. Attorney Patrick Fitzgerald—it sounded very much like Blagojevich had put Obama's seat "up for sale."

Blagojevich was certainly right about one thing: under Illinois law, the decision as to who would be the next U.S. senator from Illinois was his, and his alone, to make. Thirty-nine states give their governor the power to fill a vacant Senate seat simply by naming the individual. In eight states a special election must be held, and three states have a hybrid system of an appointment by the governor or a special election, depending on when the Senate seat becomes vacant.

Talk of who would fill Obama's vacant Senate seat had been the hottest topic of conversation among Illinois politicos during much of the summer of 2008 as it began to look as though Obama had a solid chance of winning the presidency. Some politicians, such as Congressman Jesse Jackson, Jr., were openly campaigning for the seat, while others like Congresswoman Jan Schakowsky and Congressman Danny Davis, along with five or six others, were letting it be known that they were most certainly interested. Right from the beginning, Governor Blagojevich knew he had a very big prize to hand out.

What he didn't know was that one of his closest associates, John Wyma, his chief of staff from his days in Congress—and who had become one of the state's most successful lobbyist thanks to his ties to the governor—had begun talking with Patrick Fitzgerald's investigators. Conversations had begun in October, after one of Wyma's leading clients, Provena Health, was subpoenaed to provide records about its relationship with Wyma as well as that hospital's efforts to win state approval of a new heart-care program—and a $25,000 campaign contribution to Friends of Blagojevich, given from the hospital's for-profit affiliate. The government learned from Wyma that Blagojevich was accelerating his "pay to play" fundraising schemes, attempting to bring in as much money as possible before a new state ethics law took effect in January 2009. That new legislation would limit the ability to raise money from individuals and companies that did business with the state.

Wyma refused to wear a wire to record conversations with his close friend Blagojevich, but he gave Fitzgerald's G-men enough information to enable them to ask a judge for permission to place bugs in two rooms in the offices of Friends of Blagojevich, the conference room and the governor's personal office in Chicago. The Friends of Blagojevich office held the records of the campaign fund that Robert Blagojevich, the governor's brother, had agreed to manage beginning in August 2008.

Robert Blagojevich's career had been nearly as successful, if not as public, as his younger brother's. After college, where he had gone through ROTC, he had seen the army as the best place "for a kid coming out of a lower-middle-class neighborhood to move ahead quickly, since the army is a great social equalizer." Although he was promoted to captain, had a top-secret-clearance-level job as a platoon leader at a nuclear missile unit in Germany, and was tapped to be a general's aide, Robert became frustrated with the slow-moving army bureaucracy and left for the private sector—though he did remain in the reserves, where he was promoted to lieutenant colonel. He married and had one son, settled in Nashville, Tennessee, and became an investment banker. In a Southern town like Nashville, he says, it took people a while to warm to someone with a name like Blagojevich. He taught people to say the name, a skill he passed on to his brother when he first ran for governor. His investment banking career spanned twenty years, including five years in Tampa. In 2004 he left investment banking to manage his real estate investments.

When his brother asked him to take over his fund-raising operation, Robert agreed to do it short term, just until the end of December 2008. By then the governor would be in a position to decide whether he was running again, and new fund-raising rules would prohibit contributions from those doing business with the state, making it much harder to raise money. He says he did it because "He's my brother. My brother needed help, it's that simple. No other agenda." Robert felt strongly about coming to his brother's aid because of words from his parents many years earlier: "When we're gone you will have only each other, and if you can't help each other, who are you going to help?" Robert Blagojevich makes no apologies for that decision today and says emphatically, "I've never in any way—in business, the military, dealing with government regulators, and financial services—ever had any problems with ethics."

The FBI began listening to conversations from the bugs in the Friends of Blagojevich office on October 22, 2008. They proved so productive that Fitzgerald went back to court with an unusual request to wiretap Rod Blagojevich's home phone. On the evening of October 29, investigators began intercepting calls coming into and going out from the landline in the Blagojevich home.

It was more than ironic that, just one day before Blagojevich's arrest, he told reporters, "I should say, if anybody wants to tape my conversations, go right ahead. Feel free to do it. Whatever I say is always lawful and the things I'm interested in are always lawful." He continued, "I don't believe there's any cloud that hangs over me. I think there's nothing but sunshine that hangs over me."

Hearing those remarks, Lucio Guerrero, the government's press secretary, grew concerned. "It seemed like he was egging on the feds a bit, and that scared me because you don't want to dare those guys to come and get you because they will—and they did. They did the next morning."

People wondered why Guerrero, a former newspaper reporter of Argentinean descent who had grown up in Florida, had taken the job as the embattled governor's press secretary only six months earlier. Guerrero says he believed in the governor's priorities of providing health care and implementing education, and he saw the job as a professional challenge to get the governor's story out and reshape his battered image. The job, he admits, became much more difficult on December 9.

In an afternoon news conference following the governor's morning arrest, Patrick Fitzgerald told reports that the thousands of hours of secretly taped conversations were so shocking he had little choice but to step in. "He [Blagojevich] has been arrested in the middle of what we can only describe as a political corruption crime spree. . . . We acted to stop that crime spree."

One act in that spree was most heinous, according to Fitzgerald: "The most cynical behavior in all this, the most appalling, is the fact that Governor Blagojevich tried to sell the appointment to the Senate seat vacated by President-elect Obama."

In thirty phone calls taped by the FBI between November 3 and December 5, 2008, Governor Blagojevich was heard talking to friends, fund-raisers, and advisers, about how he and his wife, Patti, could benefit financially from the Senate seat appointment. Those close to Valerie Jarrett, Barack Obama's close friend and campaign adviser, were letting it be known that she was very interested in Obama's vacant seat. On the day before the presidential election, the governor spoke with his chief of staff John Harris, Deputy Governor Bob Greenlee, and his leading outside adviser, Doug Scofield, about what Blagojevich could get in return for the Senate seat from Obama if he appointed Jarrett. Tapes caught the governor weighing the possibilities: "Unless I get something real good for [Senate Candidate 1, identified in news reports as Valerie Jarrett], shit, I'll just send myself, you know what I'm saying." And later, "I'm going to keep this Senate seat option for me a real possibility, you know, and therefore I can drive a hard bargain." Blagojevich then told Scofield that the Senate seat ". . . is a fucking valuable thing, you just don't give it away for nothing." On the day of the presidential election, Blagojevich talked with Harris, Scofield, and Greenlee about the best way to negotiate with Obama for the seat. He compared his own situation to that of a sports agent, shopping a free agent to various teams, trying to determine how much the Obama camp would offer for a Valerie Jarrett appointment, versus how much he could get from Lisa Madigan or Jesse Jackson, Jr.

The day after the election, according to taped conversations, Blagojevich began putting together a list of the government positions and private-sector jobs he might be able to obtain in exchange for the nomination of Valerie Jarrett. He talked with Deputy Governor Greenlee about the possibilities of being appointed to the president's cabinet as secretary of health and human services—or secretary of energy, which Greenlee pointed out is "the one that makes the most money." Blagojevich also began ruminating about the private sector, saying the president-elect could "put something together there . . . something big." He told Harris to look into private foundations that are "heavily dependent on federal aid," where the White House would have "influence." Once the right foundation was identified, the governor told Scofield, the president-elect could remove someone from the foundation and give the top job to Blagojevich.

Several days later another plan surfaced—to create a position for Blagojevich with an organization called Change to Win, a program sponsored by seven labor unions and aimed at improving workers' pay and benefits. Blagojevich told his advisers he needed a salary of at least $250,000 to $300,000 a year because his family was hurting financially. Tape-recorded conversations caught his advisers recommending to the governor that if Obama wanted Valerie Jarrett to have the Senate seat, Obama would have to help Blagojevich get the top job at Change to Win. Or, they said, they could try to work a three-way deal: Change to Win would trade the job it created for Blagojevich for a favor from the president-elect. A three-way deal, said Harris, would give the president-elect a "buffer so there is no obvious quid pro quo for [Jarrett]."

In a series of phone calls on November 10, Blagojevich asked his advisers about the possibility of finding a high-paying job for Patti, or placing her on paid corporate boards, in exchange for naming the president-elect's chosen candidate to the Senate. Clearly worried about his family's finances, the governor told associates that he was "struggling financially." "I want to make money," he said. Harris agreed and said they were considering what would help the "financial security" of the Blagojevich family and keep Blagojevich "politically viable." Blagojevich was not so sure he wanted to stay in politics. At one point he declared flatly that he did "not want to be governor for the next two years." But he said his consultants were telling him he had to "suck it up for two years—and do nothing and give this motherfucker [Obama] his senator. Fuck him. For nothing? Fuck him."

On November 11, Blagojevich advanced the idea of starting a 501(c)4 organization, a nonprofit entity that could engage in political activity and lobbying. The governor said President Obama could ask Warren Buffett or Bill Gates or someone like that to put $10, $12, or $15 million into the organization. Then, when Blagojevich was no longer governor, he could run it. In later taped conversations, Blagojevich continued to push that idea of a 501(c)4, which he said could be used to advocate for health care and other issues that both he and Obama cared about while he was still governor, and Jarrett could join in as a senator. Doug Scofield, the governor's adviser, told Blagojevich that he preferred the Change to Win operation. Scofield pointed out there would be fewer "fingerprints" on the president-elect's involvement since the organization already existed. Scofield said, "You won't have stories in four years that they bought you off."

Blagojevich did have a conversation with Tom Balanoff, Local #1 president of the Service Employees International Union, one of the unions behind Change to Win. Blagojevich apparently believed that Balanoff was an emissary from Valerie Jarrett to discuss her interest in the Senate seat. The governor pitched his idea of a 501(c)4 organization, which would help Jarrett as well as Blagojevich if he were to appoint her senator; and he brought up his desire to be appointed to the president's cabinet as secretary of health and human services. Balanoff agreed to "put that flag up and see where it goes."

A few days later Balanoff met with Jarrett, and both agreed that neither of Blagojevich's requests would happen. Jarrett told Balanoff it was ridiculous to think that the governor would be named to the new cabinet in the midst of several ongoing federal investigations.

At another point, Blagojevich considered appointing one of his deputy governors, identified by the news media as Louanner Peters, to fill the vacant seat. He told John Harris that if he appointed her and it began to look like he would be impeached, he could "count on [Louanner Peters]—if things got hot—to give up [the Senate seat] and let me parachute over there." But in the same conversation an increasingly frustrated Blagojevich told Harris that he knew the president-elect wanted Valerie Jarrett for the Senate seat. Angry, the governor grumbled, "They're not willing to give up anything except appreciation. Fuck them."

Blagojevich was also heard trying to "send a message to the [president-elect's] people" that Valerie Jarrett had competition for the Senate seat. Blagojevich told Guerrero to leak the name of Illinois attorney general Lisa Madigan as someone he was considering to *Chicago Sun-Times* columnist Michael Sneed. Guerrero told me in an interview that he felt it was part of his job to leak to the press, and that in this case Blagojevich wanted to "keep people unbalanced, keep them guessing to make sure there was no front-runner, to give him cover to pick up anybody he wanted to." If he had not been arrested, Guerrero thinks there was a good chance Blagojevich would have picked himself for the Senate seat.

Blagojevich's go-between with the president-elect was Congressman Rahm Emanuel. Emanuel held the seat in the U.S. House of Representatives that Blagojevich himself had held before he was elected governor. Now he was a trusted Obama adviser. He and Blagojevich remained in frequent contact. After the governor's arrest, some observers speculated that those contacts would engulf Emanuel—and even Obama—in the Senate-for-sale scandal. President-elect Obama thereupon asked his incoming White House counsel to investigate the contacts that anyone associated with Obama had had with Blagojevich and come back with a detailed report. Almost two weeks later, two days before Christmas, that report was released. It indicated there had been no inappropriate contacts between the president-elect's team and Governor Blagojevich or his people about a quid pro quo arrangement for choosing any certain person for the vacant seat. According to the report, Emanuel had had one or two telephone conversations with Blagojevich between November 6 and November 8, 2008, where he "recommended Valerie Jarrett because he knew she was interested in the seat." But, the report said, "there were no discussions of any kind of a quid pro quo for the Senate seat . . . the governor did not discuss a cabinet position . . . a private-sector position for the governor or any other personal benefit for the governor." The report also confirmed a meeting between Valerie Jarrett and Tom Balanoff but said Jarrett never understood Blagojevich's desire for a cabinet post as a quid pro quo.

The scene changed for Blagojevich on November 12 when Valerie Jarrett succumbed to pressure from the president-elect and removed herself from consideration for the Senate seat. Obama told her he would support her if she wanted the seat, but that she would be more valuable to him as a White House adviser. Blagojevich heard the news on CNN, but Chief of Staff John Harris told the governor he thought the announcement was just a tactical move by the Obama camp. That led the governor to continue discussing how he could benefit by naming Jarrett to the seat. His decision on who he should appoint, he told Harris, would be based on three criteria: "our legal situation, our personal situation, my political situation." Harris suggested to the embattled governor that his legal situation would be "the hardest one to satisfy."

Finally convinced that Jarrett really was no longer interested in the Senate seat, Blagojevich began phone conversations with his advisers about what he might get from other candidates in return for an appointment. He told his advisers that he thought he was closest to getting something from "Senate candidate 5," identified in the press as Congressman Jesse Jackson, Jr. This surprised them as Blagojevich and Jackson had had a rocky relationship since Jackson had backed out of a promised endorsement in the Democratic primary for Blagojevich's first gubernatorial campaign. By 2005 the relationship had thawed somewhat when in his State of the State Message Blagojevich promised to push for a new airport in Peotone, Illinois, forty miles south of Chicago. The proposed Abraham Lincoln National Airport in Peotone had long been a priority on Congressman Jackson's agenda. Blagojevich even invited Jackson to the State of the State Message where he sat in the front row. But a year later, when Blagojevich had failed to deliver on his promise, an angry Jackson and the fledgling airport commission launched a $250,000 ad campaign ripping into the governor for not keeping his word to support the airport.

Blagojevich, who by then was in the midst of his 2006 reelection campaign, called to arrange a meeting with

Jackson about the new airport. Encouraged, Jackson and
his communications director Rick Bryant showed up for
discussions in the luxurious Four Seasons hotel in Chicago, only to find that they would not be meeting with
Blagojevich or his chief of staff . . . but with Tony Rezko.
Rezko told Jackson and Bryant the governor would be
glad to push for their airport if he could make five of
the nine appointments to the airport board. Jackson and
Bryant were stunned by what they considered a blatant
attempt to bring pay-to-play politics to the airport board,
which was then composed of nine south suburban mayors.
Not only did Jackson turn Rezko down, he went straight
to Patrick Fitzgerald's office to report the conversation. It
would be almost two years before Jackson and Blagojevich
had any significant communication again.

Since he had no relationship with Blagojevich, Jackson
knew he would have to mount a public campaign to put
pressure on Blagojevich if he were to have a chance for
Obama's Senate seat. Jackson had been a national co-chair
of Obama's presidential campaign, had picked up the en-
dorsements of the *Chicago Sun-Times* and the *Southtown
Star* for the Senate seat, and was a front-runner in two
statewide polls when Blagojevich called him to come in
for a December 8 meeting.

Jackson says he had no idea that over a month earlier
a suburban businessman, Raghuveer Nayak, who had
been a longtime fund-raiser for Governor Blagojevich,
had hosted a luncheon where he had discussed raising
$1 million for Blagojevich if he would select Jackson for
the Senate seat. Blagojevich talked about the offer in a
conversation the FBI recorded on December 4. Said the
governor, "We were approached 'pay to play.' That . . .

you know, he'd raise me $500 grand. An emissary came. Then, the other guy would raise a million if I made him [Jesse Jackson, Jr.] a senator." The emissary was identified as Nayak, and later on December 4 Blagojevich is recorded telling his brother, Robert, that he was "elevating" Jackson because he might be able to cut a deal that would give him "something tangible up front." But, said Blagojevich, his brother should let Nayak know that "some of this stuff's gotta start happening—right now—and we gotta see it. You understand? . . . Tangible political support [campaign contributions] like you've said, 'Start showing us now.'" Robert Blagojevich said he would make the call. But the governor cautioned him: "I would do it in person. I would not do it on the phone." That warning appeared to be too late. It was the morning after Blagojevich met with Jackson in his Chicago office that the FBI moved in for his arrest.

Shortly thereafter Congressman Jackson held a news conference and denied that he had authorized anyone to ask for the governor's support on his behalf. He also said there was no mention of a quid pro quo when he met with the governor to discuss the vacant seat the night before his arrest. But there was little doubt that Jackson's dreams of becoming a U.S. senator had gone out the window with the arrest of Rod Blagojevich.

14

Quid Pro Quo

THE ATTEMPT to put President-elect Barack Obama's vacant Senate seat up for sale was the most heinous of U.S. Attorney Patrick Fitzgerald's criminal charges against Governor Rod Blagojevich. But it most certainly was not the only charge. Fitzgerald said his investigators were stunned to learn of an extortion attempt against the *Chicago Tribune*.

In 2007 Chicago real estate mogul Sam Zell had gained control of the Tribune Company, which publishes the *Chicago Tribune* and the *Los Angeles Times*, and owns the legendary baseball team the Chicago Cubs. But the purchase left Zell with a mountain of debt. In order to pay it down, he put the Cubs up for sale. The timing for a sale, however, was unfortunate: the financial markets were nearly frozen due to the failing U.S. economy.

Since private financing was so difficult, Zell had explored the idea of using the Illinois Finance Authority (IFA) as a mechanism to finance the sale of Wrigley Field.

The IFA is an economic development tool of the state, used as a conduit for private business and nonprofits to finance their projects. In the case of the Cubs, the IFA would own Wrigley Field and issue taxable municipal bonds; the Tribune Company or a new owner would receive the proceeds from the bonds and pay the debt service. Because taxable municipal bonds are viewed more favorably by investors than corporate bonds, the interest rate would be lower, saving the Tribune money.

Blagojevich thought that using the IFA to finance the deal could be worth as much as $100 million to the Tribune Company, though financial analysts say the savings would have been far less. Nevertheless the governor saw the proposed financing deal as a way to gain leverage over the *Tribune* to get what he wanted—the firing of the newspaper's editorial board. Blagojevich often complained to his staff about his treatment by the press, especially the *Tribune*. In early November 2008 he ordered John Harris to tell Zell and other *Tribune* managers that unless members of the editorial board were fired, there would be no financing deal with the IFA.

In a series of intercepted phone calls, tape-recorded by the FBI, on November 3, 2008, the governor was heard asking his deputy governor, Bob Greenlee, to check whether the *Tribune* had recently advocated that Blagojevich be impeached. In fact the *Tribune* had run an editorial that very day supporting Speaker of the House Mike Madigan's call to form a committee to consider impeachment. The November 3 editorial was just one of many, all highly critical of Blagojevich. The governor was heard on a taped phone call as he told Greenlee, "Someone should say, 'Get rid of those people!'"

The governor's wife, Patti, was heard in the background shouting to her husband to tell Greenlee "to hold up that fucking Cubs shit . . . fuck them!" Patti Blagojevich then took the phone to talk with Greenlee herself. FBI agents heard her say that Sam Zell "can just fire" the writers since he owned the paper. The governor then returned to the telephone and told Greenlee that John Harris should go to Sam Zell and tell him, "Maybe we can't do this [deal] now. Fire those fuckers!"

The governor's mood hadn't improved much the next day, November 4, when he was heard on another intercepted phone call, talking to John Harris. Blagojevich told him they needed to arrange a conversation with Sam Zell as well as with the *Tribune*'s financial adviser, Nils Larsen, and the Chicago Cubs chairman, Crane Kenney, to let them know that if the *Tribune* continued writing editorials calling for Blagojevich's impeachment, in the governor's own words, "We don't know if we can take a chance and do this IFA deal now." And one more thing, he added, "Our recommendation is fire all those fucking people, get 'em the fuck out of there—and get us some editorial support!"

Chief of Staff Harris reported back to the governor six days later that he had met with Larsen, who, he said, "got the message and is very sensitive to the issue." What's more, Harris said to Blagojevich in the tape-recorded conversation, "Certain corporate reorganizations and budget cuts are coming and—reading between the lines—he's going after that section."

"Oh, that's fantastic," Blagojevich answered.

But ten days passed and no one on the *Tribune* editorial board lost his or her job. John Harris was then heard on tape trying to convince his boss that he was in fact pushing Larsen to make it happen. But he told Blagojevich, "It's delicate—very delicate."

"I know, I know," answered Blagojevich. "Use your judgment. Don't push too hard."

Guerrero, the governor's press secretary, says it's a rare politician who does not want reporters and editorial writers fired at some point. Harris and Greenlee, he says, may have done what he frequently did: ignore the governor's more outrageous requests. "There was a lot of that in the office. A lot of people said, 'sure, okay, whatever,' and never did what the governor asked. He wanted me to call reporters all the time and complain about stories, and I never did because it just wasn't worth the fight." Guerrero says he never heard the governor ask to hold back state funds to finance a sale of Wrigley Field in exchange for firing members of the *Tribune*'s editorial board.

Ultimately no one was fired from the *Tribune* editorial board. Editorial page editor Bruce Dold says that neither he nor anyone else on the editorial board was approached by Nils Larsen or anyone in upper management about their jobs or the content of their editorials.

The bugs and wiretaps on Blagojevich's phones, plus a tap on the cell phone of the governor's close friend and fund-raiser Lon Monk, and information from Blagojevich's former congressional chief of staff, John Wyma, led to six allegations of "pay to play" politics in the federal criminal complaint that resulted in the governor's arrest. One of the schemes the feds learned about from Wyma was a threat from Blagojevich to tie up $8 million in state funds for pediatric physicians throughout Illinois. The money wouldn't be handed over, according to Wyma, until the

CEO of Chicago's Children's Memorial Hospital, Patrick Magoon, agreed to make a $50,000 contribution to the Blagojevich campaign chest. Children's Memorial is consistently ranked as one of the leading children's hospitals and research centers in the country.

According to the complaint, it was in a November 12, 2008, telephone call that Blagojevich's brother, Robert, told the governor that he had been trying to reach Magoon to talk about the contribution.

"I've left three messages there—so I'm gonna quit calling. I feel stupid now," Robert said.

"If they don't get back to you," the governor advised, "then, last resort is—I'll call."

Later that same day Blagojevich asked Bob Greenlee if the pediatric doctors' payment had been sent. Greenlee said it had not. He assured Blagojevich that the governor had total discretion over the fund. The governor mused, "We could pull it back if we needed to—budgetary concerns, right?"

"We sure could. Yep," Greenlee agreed.

"Okay. That's good to know," said the governor.

Patrick Magoon apparently successfully withstood pressure from the governor and his fund-raisers. No records indicate a contribution from Magoon or Children's Memorial Hospital in 2008.

During the Illinois House vote on the Article of Impeachment against Blagojevich, State Representative Susan Mendoza, who had led efforts to raise the Medicaid reimbursement rates for pediatric specialists who treat children from low-income families, blasted the governor. She charged him with "cynicism and hypocrisy" in attempting to hold up funding for poor children in exchange for a campaign contribution—while at the same time calling for an expansion of children's health care in Illinois.

On the day of the impeachment vote in the Illinois Senate, the $8 million in funds for pediatric specialty care for poor children was finally released. According to Rich Miller's Capitol Fax, it was the first time state funds for a program were made available without a governor's name attached.

The federal government's tape-recorded conversations played a very large role in the impeachment trial of Rod Blagojevich which began January 25, 2009. When the FBI's tape-recorded conversations of the governor's telephone calls were played in the Senate chamber, and senators heard their governor spell out the apparent shakedown of a businessman from the horse-racing industry, it marked the beginning of the end for Blagojevich.

Horse racing in Illinois had always been a big moneymaker. But the introduction of casino gambling on riverboats in Illinois hit the horse tracks hard. Track owners had been trying for years to get state legislation that would allow gaming at horse tracks. Finally in 2006 a law was passed that permitted a transfer of revenue—from Illinois' riverboat gambling casinos to the horse-racing industry. The legislation was scheduled to expire at the end of 2008, but it was given new life when the legislature, in its autumn session that year, voted to extend the provisions for another two years. The bill for renewal, worth close to $30 million for the horse-racing industry, was sitting on Blagojevich's desk when he asked Lon Monk, who had been hired by Balmoral Race Track as a lobbyist, to pressure Johnny Johnston, president of the Balmoral and Maywood tracks, for a $100,000 campaign contribution.

As the tape-recorded conversation was played at the governor's impeachment trial, the Senate chamber stilled. Then the voice of Blagojevich was heard clearly saying to Monk, "Call Johnny Johnston—or should I have Harris call him?"

Monk told Blagojevich that the governor should call Johnston. But then he reassured Blagojevich, "I'm telling you—he's gonna be good for it. I got in his face."

The state senators then heard the voice of Blagojevich's brother, Robert, telling the governor, "He's gonna give. You . . . know, he didn't get it. But he said, 'You know I'm good for it. I gotta just decide what, what . . . uh . . . accounts to get it out of.' And . . . Lon's going to talk to you about some sensitivities—legislatively—tonight when he sees you with regard to the timing of all this."

They heard the governor respond, "Right—before the end of the year though, right?" A few minutes later the governor tried to clarify the timing of the money from Johnston. "Clearly before the end of the year, right?" Blagojevich had to get the contribution before the end of the year because of the new state ethics law, scheduled to take effect January 1, 2009, that would bar political contributions from those who did business with the state.

Robert Blagojevich figured Johnston was "good for it" because he had long been one of the governor's top contributors. A February 2009 report from the National Legal and Policy Center found that interests owned or affiliated with Johnny Johnston had contributed more than $343,000 to Blagojevich's campaign committee from 2002 to 2007. But those close to Johnston say he was outraged by the latest request linking it to the horse-racing bill sitting on the governor's desk. Johnston considered the request a shakedown and never contributed the $100,000. Blagojevich finally signed the racetrack legislation on December 15, 2008, one week after his arrest.

Patrick Fitzgerald, at his press conference following the governor's arrest, called Blagojevich's conduct so appalling it "would make Lincoln roll over in his grave." The arrest, he said, was a "moment of truth for Illinois . . . a time to confront the wide-ranging corruption that has plagued the state for so long." Fitzgerald was doing his part to rid Illinois government of corruption. He asked the citizens of Illinois to do their part as well—to come forward with any information that might make them think, "This is not how you run a government." Fitzgerald later reported to a federal judge that so many citizens had taken him up on his offer that he asked the court for four additional months to prepare a criminal indictment against Rod Blagojevich.

15

Fallout: A New Senator

THE CHARGES leveled against Governor Rod Blagojevich in Patrick Fitzgerald's criminal complaint stunned the political world, not just in Illinois but across the nation. Political corruption was scarcely a new phenomenon in Illinois, but "selling a Senate seat" or "shaking down a children's hospital"—that was simply beyond the bounds of what most citizens or even shady politicians could tolerate. There was also amazement that the governor would have talked about such deals over the telephone when he knew the United States attorney had him in his sights.

Following his appearance before Judge Jan Nolan in federal court after his arrest on December 9, 2008, Blagojevich was sneaked out the back entrance of the Dirksen Building in downtown Chicago to avoid the hordes of reporters and cameras waiting in the lobby. The scene outside his northwest side home was the same—a crush of reporters, lights, and cameras. The quiet residential neighborhood was transformed into a war zone of sorts, the rumble of satellite television truck engines and swirling news helicopters overhead sounding like machine guns. (After several weeks of this kind of nonstop coverage, Patti Blagojevich wrote a note to her neighbors apologizing for the noise and congestion.)

Inside the house the Blagojeviches adopted a bunker-like mentality. They could not leave without being accosted by the press, so they hunkered down and stayed inside. It was the hardest on twelve year-old Amy. Her father had been governor for half her life, and she was often in tears, concerned that he would no longer be the governor and trying to understand how all their lives had changed so quickly on December 9, a day Blagojevich referred to as the family's personal Pearl Harbor day. Annie too had crying bouts, and both girls had trouble sleeping. Wanting to hold onto some stability in their routine, the girls continued going to school. Amy's teacher was particularly sensitive to her feelings. On the day of the arrest she pulled Amy out of class and took her to her own home to bake cookies and get her away from all the talk about her father. Trying to cheer up his daughters, the governor brought home a dog, which the girls instantly fell in love with. Friends urged the family to get away, to take a vacation and leave the madness behind. But Patti Blagojevich thought her daughters would be better off in their own beds. They did take up her father's offer of a weekend at his home in Lake Geneva, a place Patti and the girls loved. Dick Mell did not join them.

When Blagojevich wanted to leave, other than going out to jog or to work, he sneaked out. According to Lucio Guerrero, "He had this elaborate scheme of going next door, jumping the back fence, then meeting up with his security detail farther down the alley. It was insane, but he liked that game, you know. He liked the cat-and-mouse game with the media."

While Blagojevich wasn't talking, fellow politicians had plenty to say. Calls for his resignation began immediately. Illinois lieutenant governor Pat Quinn called a press conference before Blagojevich had even left the Dirksen Building. Quinn asked the governor "to do the right thing and step aside," adding that Blagojevich was "seriously impeded from carrying out his oath of office."

Illinois' senior senator Dick Durbin quickly sent a letter on his Senate stationery with a personal plea to the governor to step down. Wrote Durbin, "I urge you to search your heart and summon the strength to put your state and your nation above any personal consideration."

Initially most of Blagojevich's colleagues thought he *would* resign after being publicly humiliated by his early-morning arrest. The criminal charges in Fitzgerald's complaint were so devastating that it seemed unimaginable that Blagojevich could continue. No politician in the country had ever recovered from such accusations without resigning or being thrown out of office.

Blagojevich's staff thought he would resign and had a resignation speech ready for him two days after the arrest, though they were as stunned by the turn of events as everyone else, says Lucio Guerrero. "We were all in shock at the office. I mean, the office was to me the walking dead—nobody knew what would happen next. The feds had come in, my computer was taken, Greenlee's computer was taken, and other people's computers were taken. So it was scary, it was really scary."

Many on the staff were also angry. "If he didn't resign, they wanted him at least to step aside, and they were angry he didn't do that because it affected *their* lives. We were all vulnerable. If he'd have stepped aside, we might have been able to keep our jobs or at least work with the new administration, but now we all get the taint of it. I was loyal to some of his policies, but I was angry that he got us into this mess." But the governor had no intention of resigning and never read the prepared resignation speech.

Soon calls for Blagojevich's resignation turned to outcries for his impeachment and removal from office. Impeachment of the governor had in fact been talked about in the Illinois legislature for nearly a year. Speaker of the House Mike Madigan had already drawn up a list of talking points for impeachment, which had been leaked to the media. The talking points set out three bases for impeaching the governor: the ongoing criminal investigation that directly implicated him; abusing the power of his office by evading the legislative prerogatives of the General Assembly; and acting as an absentee governor by rarely showing up at his office in Chicago or Springfield. Still, legislators were nervous about what many of them considered to be the "nuclear option"—removing an elected governor.

Only one Illinois official had ever been impeached by the Illinois House of Representatives. In the 1830s a justice of the Illinois Supreme Court, Theophilus Smith, was accused of running amok. Even after his impeachment, the trial in the Illinois Senate resulted in an acquittal, and the judge remained on the bench.

But U.S. Attorney Fitzgerald's criminal complaint poured gasoline on a fire that was already burning. Democrats as well as Republicans suggested that the time had come to consider impeachment proceedings. "Today our state is facing a crisis," said House Republican leader Tom Cross. He called for impeachment hearings to begin immediately in the Illinois House, saying, "Illinois citizens are victims of a corrupt governor." And on December 15, 2008, the Illinois House launched its first-ever impeachment probe of a governor.

Three days earlier Attorney General Lisa Madigan, who had her eye on the governorship herself and did not care to wait for an impeachment process to oust the governor, asked the Illinois Supreme Court for a temporary restraining order that would remove the governor from office, citing his "political disability." "It is absolutely clear," Madigan said, "that the governor is incapable of governing."

Madigan's unprecedented request put the highest court in Illinois in very unfamiliar territory. The Illinois constitution has provisions for removing a governor for reasons of death, resignation, or other disability. Lisa Madigan argued that Blagojevich had a *political* disability and could no longer govern effectively. In just five days the court rejected that argument, leaving Blagojevich in the governor's office.

Lieutenant Governor Quinn, Senator Durbin, and Attorney General Madigan—and nearly all the rest of Illinois' Democratic politicians—did agree on one aspect of the governor's situation: after federal charges were filed against him, they did not want Blagojevich choosing a replacement for Barack Obama's vacant Senate seat. In Senator Durbin's letter to Blagojevich he asked him explicitly "not to appoint the next United States Senator from Illinois." Durbin wrote, "Because of the nature of the charges against you, no matter whom you were to select, that individual would be under a cloud of suspicion." Durbin's efforts also produced a letter from Democratic Senate Majority Leader Harry Reid—and signed by all fifty members of the Senate Democratic caucus—telling Blagojevich, "We write to insist that you step down as Governor of Illinois and under no circumstances make an appointment to fill the vacant Illinois Senate seat." Senator Reid's letter went on to say that if Blagojevich ignored the request and made a Senate appointment, the Senate would exercise its right to decide not to seat that individual. Both Durbin and Quinn called for a special election to fill the seat to avoid any taint on a new senator.

As the rhetoric escalated, Blagojevich remained quiet, establishing some semblance of a daily work routine, surrounded by the media in every public moment. He did not abandon his early-morning run, bounding through Chicago's snow-covered streets in his black jogging suit at a pace of eight minutes and fifteen seconds per mile. He made it hard for panting reporters and gear-laden cameramen to keep up with him, much less get a question answered—though several tried. When his run was complete, the governor would reenter his house, eventually to reemerge in his business suit, hop into a black SUV, and be driven by an Illinois state trooper to the governor's office in the State of Illinois Building in Chicago's Loop. More than one observer noted that Rod Blagojevich spent more time in the governor's office after the criminal charges were filed than he had in the entire preceding year.

He also spent time building his legal defense team beyond his old friend Sheldon Sorosky. He added Ed Genson, a legal legend in Chicago, whose list of clients included distinguished figures as well as crooked politicians, mobsters, newspaper publishers, and rock stars. Genson had represented R&B singer R. Kelly, accused of child pornography, and won an acquittal—his most recent high-profile success. Genson suffers from a neurological disorder that requires him to use an electric scooter to get around. But his physical disability has never cost him a beat when it comes to putting together a tough defense for his clients. He is a rumpled, roly-poly man who is the antithesis of the slick-talking defense lawyer. Blagojevich also brought on board the father-and-son team of Sam Adam Jr. and Sr. The Adams were leading criminal defense attorneys who often paired with Genson on important cases. Sam Adam Jr. had played a key role in the acquittal of R. Kelly.

Finally, ten days after his arrest and four days after impeachment proceedings had begun in Springfield, Blagojevich broke his silence. He called a news conference. Media and politicians alike attended on the assumption that the governor would announce his resignation. But when Blagojevich walked into the room, it was the defiant, unapologetic, former Golden Gloves boxer who stood at the podium in the media room in the Thompson Center. The governor put his hands on the lectern, looked around the room, and said, "I am here to tell you—right off the bat—that I am *not guilty* of any criminal wrongdoing. I intend to *stay* on the job. I will fight this thing every step of the way. I will *fight*. I will *fight*. I will *fight*—every step of the way until I take my last breath. I have done nothing wrong."

The news conference was vintage Blagojevich. He portrayed himself as being under attack from "powerful forces" and "political enemies" who were trying to take away the office the people had given him. He declared, "I'm not going to quit a job the people hired me to do because of false accusations and a political lynch mob."

The governor addressed none of the charges in the federal criminal complaint. Instead he vowed to take his case to the courts, saying, "And when I do, I am absolutely certain that I will be vindicated." Then he reached back to his favorite Kipling poem to close the news conference.

If you can keep your head when all about you
Are losing theirs and blaming it on you,
If you can trust yourself when all men doubt you
[But] make allowance for their doubting too . . .

The governor's statement lasted three minutes. He took no questions.

Rod Blagojevich had thrown down the gauntlet. He would not heed the calls to resign. He would not slink away as a disgraced politician. Instead he insisted he was innocent and vowed to fight for his political life in every way he could.

Once again the state's public officials were flabbergasted. "Wake up—the people are in jeopardy," said Lieutenant Governor Quinn. "And the governor needs to realize that. It's time to step aside." Republican state senator Matt Murphy, who became one of the leaders in the impeachment fight, noted, "We heard '*fight, fight, fight*' instead of '*resign, resign, resign.*' This governor has lost his ability to lead."

When it became clear that Blagojevich would not resign, concern heightened over the selection to fill Obama's vacant Senate seat. Always the populist, Blagojevich, who was still the governor, let it be known that if a bill landed on his desk calling for a special election, he would indeed sign it. But after weighing the possibilities, Democrats retreated from their early calls for a special election. They feared that the Blagojevich scandals might make for a Republican victory in such an election. The November general election had left the U.S. Senate nearly split, with two seats—Minnesota and Alaska—still being counted, and no clear majority for either party. Republicans at both the state and national levels were salivating at the possibility of picking up not just a Republican seat but the seat of the incoming Democratic president.

Illinois legislators were reassured, however, by a statement from Blagojevich's high-powered lawyer, Ed Genson. The governor, he said, would not make the Senate appointment. And so the full Illinois House adjourned until mid-January, effectively ending the possibility of a special election to fill the seat.

The politicians should have known better. Although Genson was advising Blagojevich against naming a replacement for Obama, Guerrero and other leading staffers thought he should make the appointment. "Once the General Assembly decided not to pass the bill that would have called for a special election," says Guerrero, "he was like, 'This is the final fuck you. I'm going to do it.' And I was for that because I thought if you are going to say it's business as usual, and as the governor I'm signing bills and doing clemency, well then you have to do this too."

There was also a disagreement between Blagojevich's lawyers. While Genson was counseling against an appointment, Sam Adam Jr. was all for it, and he had a candidate in mind: Roland Burris. Blagojevich liked the idea of Burris. Although Burris had been his opponent in the

2002 gubernatorial primary, he had been a loyal supporter and contributor after Blagojevich became governor. Burris had let it be known early on that he would like the appointment to replace Obama, and that got him into trouble after he was sworn in as a new senator when questions arose of "pay to play" in his appointment. But those troubles were in the future on the night of December 28, 2008, when Adam Jr. called Burris to ask him if he would accept the governor's appointment as new U.S. senator. Burris had not been Blagojevich's first choice. Congressman Danny Davis, an African American from Chicago's West Side, had turned down the appointment, saying he was worried about the taint from the governor's criminal and political problems.

Few knew any of this when, on the day before New Year's Eve, Blagojevich swept into the crowded press room in the Thompson Center from a side door, showing few signs of stress, wearing a crisp white shirt, his trademark hair lacquered in place, and stepped to the podium. By this time the Blagojevich story had gone national and even international, bringing at least twenty camera crews with reporters from around the country. "The people of Illinois are entitled to have two United States Senators represent them in Washington, D.C.," he began. "As governor, I am required to make this appointment. If I don't make this appointment, then the people of Illinois will be deprived of their appropriate voice and vote in the United States Senate."

He smiled briefly at the elegant-looking, African-American man of small stature standing next to him. Blagojevich said, "So I'm here today to announce that I am appointing Roland Burris as the next United States

Senator from Illinois." Before he yielded the podium to Burris, he added, "And now, I'd like to ask everyone to do one last thing. Please don't allow the allegations against me to taint this good and honest man."

Rockin' Rod had once again demonstrated his self-proclaimed "testicular virility." Democrats would still have to deal with the man they had pronounced all but dead. "Admit it," wrote *Chicago Sun-Times* columnist Carol Marin, "it was a brilliant move."

Roland Burris, a seventy-one-year-old veteran politician, was a choice difficult to oppose. Some may have viewed him as a washed-up politician with an oversized ego after his defeats in three races for governor and one for mayor of Chicago. But Burris had some firepower of his own. He had been the first African American elected to statewide office in Illinois when he won the post of state comptroller in 1979, and he was reelected to two more terms. He again benefited from his statewide popularity in 1991 with a win as Illinois attorney general.

Just as important in the toxic climate in which Blagojevich named Burris for the Senate seat, it was to his credit that to that point Burris had *never* been on the wrong side of the law in his political life, much less the subject of an indictment from the U.S. attorney's office. His small stature did not hide an oversized ego, best epitomized by the large mausoleum emblazoned with the words "Trail Blazer" that sat ready for Burris in one of Chicago's most historic cemeteries. There was still room to carve U.S. SENATOR on one of the three large stone panels under two stately columns. Aside from the annoying habit of using the royal "we," when referring to himself—"We will deal with the next step in the process"—Roland Burris was effective on the political stump and had a strong base in the African-American community. It would be difficult for Blagojevich's enemies to oppose this likable, popular man to fill the vacant Senate seat.

A beaming Burris told those assembled at the news conference, "I accept this appointment to fill the unexpired term of President-elect Barack Obama."

It was difficult to imagine how this event might get even stranger, but Congressman Bobby Rush then emerged from the back of the room and walked to the microphones. In the 1960s Rush had been a Chicago leader of the radical Black Panthers. Later he had mellowed, turned to traditional politics, and in 1992 was elected to the United States Congress from the First District of Illinois. He soon became of the strongest and most respected leaders in Chicago's large African-American community. A few years earlier, in 2000, Rush had demonstrated his substantial political muscle in an election in which he walloped by a two-to-one margin a young state senator named Barack Obama who challenged him for his congressional seat.

Congressman Rush was fighting throat cancer when he stepped to the podium to address the assembled reporters. His voice was soft and raspy. But as he spoke, his message couldn't have been heard louder or clearer. He argued that the Senate seat left vacant by President-elect Obama must be filled by an African American. To do anything else would leave the United States Senate without a single African-American member.

His words were challenging. "I would ask you," he said, "to not hang or lynch the appointee as you try to castigate the appointer." To make sure those U.S. senators who had vowed not to seat *anyone* appointed by Blagojevich understood just how high the race-based political stakes were, Rush issued this warning: "I don't think that any U.S. senator that's sitting in the Senate right now wants to go on record to deny one African American from being seated in the U.S. Senate."

Strong though they were, Rush's words left Senate Democrats unbowed. They issued a statement once again insisting that anyone appointed by the tainted governor would *not* be seated by the Democratic Caucus. Even President-elect Obama backed the senators' decision, saying, "Roland Burris is a good man and fine public servant, but the Senate Democrats made it clear weeks ago that they cannot accept an appointment made by a governor who is accused of selling this very Senate seat."

It was left to the Illinois secretary of state, Jesse White, to fire the first official shot against the Burris appointment. White, also an African American, had been at odds with Rod Blagojevich since the governor's first-term budget mandates. But White maintained that this was not what led him to refuse to sign the document necessary to certify Burris's appointment. White maintained, "I did not want to affix my signature to a document put forth by a gentleman who I thought had the possibility of being impeached, the possibility of being indicted, out on bond, who got caught trying to sell the office that he was trying to make an appointment to. So I just didn't want to be associated with him in any shape, form, or fashion."

As the battle raged over the seating of Roland Burris in the United States Senate, the Sunday morning talk shows debated Chicago's race-based politics, the story spilling out across the national airwaves. On NBC's *Meet the Press,* Senate Majority Leader Harry Reid denied reports that in a telephone call with Rod Blagojevich he had expressed doubts about the future electability of three African Americans who had expressed interest in the vacant Senate seat—Chicago congressmen Jesse Jackson, Jr., and Danny Davis, and Illinois State Senate president Emil Jones. Reid called the accusation "spin" from the "obviously corrupt" governor of Illinois. Reid denied he had told Blagojevich whom *not to appoint.* And on ABC's *This Week with George Stephanopoulos,* Illinois' senior senator Dick Durbin continued to insist that Roland Burris would not be seated as the junior senator from Illinois.

Meanwhile Roland Burris and his supporters were ignoring the opposition to his appointment. At a Sunday evening prayer service on Chicago's South Side, Burris declared, "I am now the junior senator from the State of Illinois. Some people wanted to doubt that. That is their right."

Congressman Rush, organizer of the prayer service, continued to accuse Senate Democrats of racial motives in their refusal to seat Burris, calling the Senate "one of the last bastions of plantation and racial politics in America." Senate Democrats who would not seat Burris, Rush declared, were "going to have to come and ask for forgiveness" from black America—not surprising words from someone who had battled for equal rights for more than half a century.

But it was ironic that this battle was being waged in Illinois. It was Illinois, after all, that had sent two of only three African Americans to the U.S. Senate in modern times—Carol Moseley Braun, Barack Obama, and now Roland Burris. And the people of Illinois had worked hard to help Barack Obama win the presidency.

The president-elect was in fact growing increasingly concerned that the uproar over Burris's appointment was distracting from his efforts to craft a smooth transition to the White House. Still, for the moment Obama continued to support the Democratic Caucus in its determination to keep Burris from taking Obama's former Senate seat.

Roland Burris remained undaunted. On opening day of the new Congress, January 6, 2009—a cold, dreary, and rainy morning in Washington—Burris arrived at the Capitol to present his credentials as Illinois' new senator. Throngs of reporters and camera crews documented his every move. But the hopeful Burris was turned away from the Senate chambers. He retreated graciously to a small park nearby. Sheltered from the rain beneath a large black umbrella, he told reporters, "My name is Roland Burris, the junior senator from the State of Illinois. I was advised that my credentials were not in order."

MSNBC's Chris Matthews called the images of Burris being turned away "akin to the pictures of attacks on early civil rights protesters in the 1960s." But just one week later the scene changed completely. With a push from the president-elect, Senate Democrats began to realize they did not have a legal leg to stand on in their opposition to seating Burris. Illinois secretary of state Jesse White continued to refuse to sign a certificate of election—but he did sign a document indicating that Governor Blagojevich had appointed Roland Burris to the U.S. Senate. And after all, Rod Blagojevich, despite all his legal woes, was still governor of the State of Illinois, with constitutional authority to appoint someone to fill a vacancy in the U.S. Senate.

I asked Jesse White how he felt about being asked to sign the second document. He replied, "I described their actions as 'strap-me-into-a-wheelchair-and-roll-me-down-four-flights-of-stairs.'"

After exhausting all possibilities to block the appointment of Roland Burris, Senate Democrats, led by Harry Reid and Dick Durbin, suddenly found his paperwork acceptable. On January 15 Burris put his right hand on a Bible and was sworn in as the junior senator from Illinois.

Rod Blagojevich had outfoxed his opponents by installing his own choice to replace Barack Obama. But it would be his last political victory.

16

Impeached

JUST SIX DAYS after Rod Blagojevich was taken away
in handcuffs in the early morning hours from his Chicago
home, lawmakers in the Illinois House of Representatives
voted overwhelmingly—114 for impeachment, 1 against,
and 1 vote of "present"—to authorize the first-ever impeachment trial of a sitting governor in the state.

Impeachment trials are rare in the United States at
both the federal and state levels. There is a strong reluctance in a democratic nation to undo what the voters have
done. Only eleven U.S. governors have been impeached,
and only seven of them were removed from office.

Illinois legislators were well aware of the momentous
nature of the action they were about to undertake, one
made more difficult by the Illinois constitution's lack of a
clear definition of the grounds for impeachment. The U.S.
Constitution specifies that "The President, Vice President,
and all civil officers of the United States, shall be removed
from office on impeachment, and conviction of, treason,

bribery, or other high crimes and misdemeanors." But in Illinois the only guidelines are hazy, stating that executive and judicial officers may be impeached if the House of Representatives can determine the existence of cause for impeachment.

As Illinois House members on the newly formed Special Investigative Committee met on December 17, 2008, in a hearing room in the ornate state capitol in Springfield, they vowed to develop a fair and impartial impeachment process, despite the history of many legislators' distrust of Blagojevich. Christmas carols rang through the capitol rotunda as children from a rural grade school sang for their appreciative parents just outside the hearing room. And inside, twenty-one committee members sat in a banked row of desks, facing witness tables at the front of the room. Representative Lou Lang addressed the question of whether his colleagues could hold impartial hearings after years of leveling harsh criticism at the governor. "There are many in this committee room who have been critical of this governor on a number of issues, but this committee must do its deliberations without regard to politics, without regard to differences of public policy, and even without regard to whether the governor is competent and whether he's done his job well. It must only be about whether the governor has violated his constitutional oath," said Lang.

Although he stayed out of the limelight as always, Blagojevich's nemesis, House Speaker Mike Madigan, had firm control of the Investigative Committee. His chief lieutenant, House Majority Leader Barbara Flynn Currie, was installed as chairwoman, and Madigan's legal counsel, David Ellis, acted as counsel to the committee. Currie too insisted the committee hearings would be fair. "This is not a kangaroo court. It's absolutely critical that we do this deliberately—that we don't rush to judgment, that we don't say, because the public is clamoring for his head, we should take the head first and do the trial later," she told committee members.

Representing the governor before the Investigative Committee were his newly hired lawyers, Ed Genson and Sam Adam, Jr.

After just one day on the job as Blagojevich's attorney, Genson was already questioning the motives of the Investigative Committee. "Everybody's in a rush to judgment," he told reporters. "If you know of another case coming out of the State of Illinois that had more pizzazz to it—where there were so many people that wanted to chop somebody's head off—you tell me it. But I don't. This is a real witch hunt." Genson's strategy was clearly to put the legislators on the defensive.

Operating much like a grand jury in a criminal case, it was the newly formed committee's job to investigate the governor's activities—to determine if there was indeed cause to draw up an Article of Impeachment, which would resemble an indictment in a criminal trial. If they did, it would then require a vote of at least 60 of the 118 members of the House to move the Article of Impeachment to the Illinois Senate. There a trial would be held to determine if the governor should be removed from office.

The Investigative Committee hearings opened with evidence from the federal criminal complaint, which had been filed in federal court by U.S. Attorney Patrick Fitzgerald against Governor Blagojevich and his chief of staff, John Harris. It was this criminal complaint that had galvanized the legislature to act, even though several legislators had been trying for years to figure out how to bring impeachment proceedings against the governor.

The federal complaint itself was just two pages, charging Blagojevich and Harris with one count each of using mail and wire communications to defraud the State of Illinois and its citizens of their honest services; and a second count of corruptly soliciting the *Chicago Tribune* to fire its editorial board members in exchange for a financial benefit from the State of Illinois. It was the accompanying seventy-six page affidavit, compiled by FBI agent Daniel Cain and filed by Fitzgerald, that contained the explosive charges. The allegations included trying to "sell" the U.S. Senate seat recently held by Barack Obama—for an asking price of more than a million dollars. It also accused the governor of trying to shake down Children's Memorial Hospital in Chicago by withholding financial assistance intended to pay for health care for poor children across the state. Blagojevich was charged with soliciting the owner of two Chicago area racetracks for $100,000 in return for financial aid for the cash-strapped horse-racing industry. Fitzgerald had also accused the governor of corrupting two state boards, the Illinois Finance Authority and the Teachers' Retirement System. In short, Blagojevich was accused of promising to deliver state contracts or financial aid in exchange for campaign contributions—which, in Illinois political terms, was dubbed "pay to play."

Most of the committee members were already familiar with the federal charges. But the mood in the committee room grew somber, with some members shaking their heads in disbelief, as they heard the committee's counsel recite the shocking allegations.

But Ed Genson, representing the governor, insisted the federal criminal complaint should not be admitted as evidence in the State Senate's impeachment proceeding, because it was just that—a complaint. It was not even an indictment, Genson argued, much less a conviction, and was therefore unproven. As for the secretly recorded wiretaps that made up much of the evidence in the complaint, Genson told the committee that it would be a violation of due process to include them since the governor had no access to the original tapes or transcripts—no way to know if the quotes were accurate, no way to know if they had been "cherry picked" in a way that changed their meaning.

And, said the defense attorney, "There's no evidence in the complaint that proves that any illegal acts took place. There's nothing on that tape that shows that people were asked to give money, or campaign contributions, or anything. It's just talk. That's what it is—unfortunate talk. Talk that was talk—that shouldn't have been made, perhaps—but not actions."

The only names associated with the wiretaps in the criminal complaint, Genson argued, were those of the defendants, Rod Blagojevich and John Harris. All others were referred to by a virtual alphabet soup of numbers and letters, *Fund-raiser A, Individual A, Lobbyist 1,* and so on. "If you don't know the names of the people in the complaint," said Genson, "these are shadows, and we are—we are, with regard to these allegations—fighting shadows, and that's not right. That's not clear and convincing evidence."

Genson sparred repeatedly with committee members over the governor's right to call witnesses to testify at the hearing. Without that ability, Genson said, there could be no due process. Blagojevich's lawyer was repeatedly rebuffed. Committee Chairwoman Currie and other members of the panel argued that they were not engaged in a *criminal* proceeding. They contended that the governor's guilt or innocence was not at stake. "We do not have to find the governor guilty of a criminal offense in order to decide if he is guilty of something impeachable," said Currie.

Only Chairwoman Currie had the ability to subpoena witnesses, and that was subject to the approval of Speaker of the House Madigan, a rule that angered Republicans on the committee but one they ultimately accepted. And the committee unanimously agreed that they would not subpoena any witness who would interfere with the criminal case being conducted by Patrick Fitzgerald.

In a letter to Fitzgerald, the committee asked for guidance as to whom they could subpoena or ask to appear without jeopardizing his case. Fitzgerald responded that taking testimony from anyone related to the allegations in the criminal complaint "could significantly compromise the ongoing criminal investigation." Attorney Genson contended that the committee was not bound by Fitzgerald's desire to prove his criminal case against Rod Blagojevich. If the committee was seeking to remove the governor from office, Genson argued, Blagojevich ought to be able to bring in witnesses to prove that the allegations leveled against him in the criminal complaint were not true.

The governor's lawyer particularly wanted to bring in Congressman Rahm Emanuel and Valerie Jarrett, both of whom had already been named as key aides to President-elect Obama. Genson introduced into evidence the report by incoming White House counsel Greg Craig, which exonerated Emanuel and Jarrett of being involved in any quid pro quo discussions with regard to "selling" Obama's Senate seat. But Emanuel and Jarrett were on Fitzgerald's "do not call" list, and Genson's request was denied.

The Investigative Committee did call in witnesses to testify about noncriminal charges, instances where the committee believed the governor had abused the power of his office. The most significant of these was the governor's expansion of Family Care health insurance over the objections of the legislative rules committee, the JCAR. Blagojevich, the committee charged, had gone around the JCAR to establish his health-care initiative after he could not get the bill through the legislature.

Witnesses called by the Investigative Committee were also questioned about the governor's decision to purchase flu vaccine from England in 2004—vaccine that was never actually delivered to Illinois—and his I-Save-Rx prescription drug program, which allowed Illinois citizens to purchase drugs in Canada, which legislators maintained was illegal.

Witnesses testified that the governor did not follow a legal appropriations process when allocating money for the state's Agency Efficiency Initiatives, an administrative program that was supposed to restructure the state's business procedures. And they maintained that he had violated both state and federal laws in the hiring and firing of various state employees.

Ed Genson chose to call no witnesses to rebut the noncriminal charges. He contended that those charges amounted to political and policy disputes, not impeachable offenses. And all the disputes, with the exception of the expansion of Family Care, had occurred in Blagojevich's first term. Therefore, Genson said, they were irrelevant since voters had approved the governor's actions by re-electing him in 2006.

Many on the governor's staff and in his cabinet wanted the governor to fight back and were angry about the decision not to present a defense for the noncriminal charges. Hours had been spent preparing an impeachment defense for the governor that laid out the legal justification for the expansion of health care and the importing of prescription drugs and vaccine, programs that were at the heart of the Blagojevich agenda and to which most of his staff had been strongly committed. According to Lucio Guerrero, "If it was up to the staff we would have been there day one defending it, because it made the staff look bad. It made us look like we were reckless." But attorneys Genson and Adam Jr. stuck to their decision to call no witnesses, and the staff work on the impeachment defense was never used.

The one witness Genson could have called to rebut all the charges was Rod Blagojevich himself. The committee repeatedly challenged him to bring the governor in to testify. "If you want the facts, bring [the governor] here," one agitated state representative stormed. "Let's ask the questions. There's a lot of things we'd like to know."

Genson asked committee members to respect Blagojevich's right against self-incrimination as he was facing an upcoming criminal trial. And he cautioned the committee not to react negatively because the governor did not appear. Once again, panel members responded that since the impeachment was not a criminal trial, the governor's silence *could* be taken into account. Finally, Genson blasted the panel for not laying out standards for what constituted impeachment. He contended that the federal criminal complaint should not be included in any Article of Impeachment because witnesses could not be called to prove or disprove the charges. As for the noncriminal charges, he reiterated that they did not reach the level of impeachable offenses. But the committee concluded in its final report that the only standard of impeachment in Illinois was "cause." The report declared, "It's up to each individual member to decide what constitutes 'cause' for impeachment."

The committee decided that the governor's repeated abuse of power in fact amounted to "cause." The governor, the committee found, was no longer capable of governing, citing two examples that had occurred after the governor's arrest. The U.S. Department of Homeland Security had revoked the governor's access to classified security information, and the governor's arrest had led to a downgrading of state bonds, which cost Illinois nearly $21 million in added interest payments.

After seven days of hearings, the Investigative Committee was ready to vote. A solemn Representative Lou Lang addressed the committee: "This is a grave and sobering time . . . we have had to answer: Has the governor violated his constitutional oath? . . . The constitution only refers to cause [as the standard for impeachment] . . . the evidence introduced in this Committee meets any standard of cause."

The governor's longtime critic, Representative Jack Franks, held nothing back. "I believe Rod Blagojevich is a liar!" he said. "I believe Rod Blagojevich is a thief! He violated ethics laws, court orders—and has driven our state to the abyss . . . the governor ought to resign. He should spare himself from being the only governor in Illinois history to be impeached." By a vote of 21 to 0, the Special Investigative Committee recommended that the full House consider an Article of Impeachment against Governor Rod Blagojevich.

The following day—on what would have been the ninety-fifth birthday of Rod Blagojevich's hero, Richard Nixon—the Illinois House convened to consider the impeachment of the governor. The usual chatter of members kibitzing in the aisles of the House chamber was absent. The visitors' galleries were filled, but across the crowded room, faces were solemn. The air in the chamber was heavy with the responsibility of serious business. Speaker Michael Madigan stood at the lectern at precisely nine o'clock in the morning and called the House to order.

Majority Leader Barbara Flynn Currie began laying out the evidence compiled by the Special Investigative Committee that resulted in a thirteen-point Article of Impeachment. The first eight points related to the criminal complaint—plotting to "sell" the Senate seat; plotting to withhold state assistance to the *Tribune* unless editors were fired; engaging in "pay-to-play" schemes involving the horse-racing industry, tollway contactors, children's hospitals, Ali Ata and the Illinois Finance Authority, Joe Cari and the Teachers' Retirement System Board, and the Illinois Health Facilities Planning Board. The remaining five points related to the governor's abuse of power in unlawfully expanding the Family Care program; unapproved purchase of flu vaccine; unapproved importation of prescription drugs from Canada; violating the appropriations process; and violating state and federal hiring laws. "This governor has violated his oath of office. This governor has breached the public trust. This governor must be impeached," Currie pleaded.

For ninety minutes House members, Republicans and Democrats, lashed out at the governor's behavior. Not a single member rose in his defense. Even his longtime friend and floor leader, Representative Jay Hoffman, kept his silence.

"Rod Blagojevich, you should be ashamed of yourself," said Chicago Democratic Representative Susana Mendoza, her voice rising. "But I won't pretend to think you feel any! You've already shown us you have none! So take your sullied place in history. And I hope your fate serves as a notice for any other public official who even has a fleeting thought of following your example—that they will be held accountable as well."

The two electronic voting boards high on the chamber walls told the story. The vote was 114 to 1 in favor of sending a thirteen-point Article of Impeachment against Governor Rod Blagojevich to the Illinois Senate.

Barbara Flynn Currie said the reality of the moment stunned her. She remembered, "I thought, oh my God!—the governor is impeached! This is very tough stuff—to undo a fair, free, open election, the cornerstone of our democracy—to overturn the results of an election is just wrenching."

17

Removal

ON THE MORNING of the vote to impeach, the governor took refuge in the two things that sustained him, running and literature. As the "yes" votes were piling up in Springfield, Blagojevich was racking up the miles in his Chicago neighborhood. His run completed, he told the waiting media gaggle, "I feel like the old Alan Sillitoe short story 'The Loneliness of the Long Distance Runner.'" He may have forgotten that the hero of the story is a petty criminal who finds solace in running and eventually winds up competing on the track team of a juvenile detention facility.

Three and a half hours after the vote to impeach him, Blagojevich was ready to hold a press conference. It was the beginning of what would become an all-out media blitz to proclaim his innocence and attack his persecutors, the Illinois legislature. The defiant governor told reporters that the impeachment vote was a "foregone conclusion" from legislators who had opposed his efforts to work for the best interests of the people of Illinois. Surrounded by a group of Illinois voters, several in wheelchairs, Blagojevich proclaimed, "From the moment of my reelection I have been engaged in a struggle to get things done for people." While not responding to any of the charges in the Article of Impeachment, the governor insisted, "I am not guilty of any criminal wrongdoing. I am confident that at the end of the day I will be properly exonerated. . . . I am going to fight this every step of the way."

He then turned to his second-favorite nineteenth-century British poet, Alfred Lord Tennyson, to conclude his remarks: "*We are not now the strength which in old days / Moved earth and heaven, that which we are, we are. / One equal temper of heroic hearts, made weak by time and by fate, but strong in will, / To strive, to seek, to find. And not to yield.*" The unrepentant, poetry-reading governor received good billing on all the national news shows.

While Blagojevich was quoting poetry, his lawyers were dealing with Patrick Fitzgerald's criminal complaint. In early January 2009 the lawyers took the bold step of asking a federal judge to remove Fitzgerald from the Blagojevich corruption case. The U.S. attorney's December 9, 2008, press conference announcing the criminal complaint against Blagojevich had raised eyebrows in the legal community. Barry Coburn, a former prosecutor, writing in the *New York Times*, observed, "It is hard to feel comfortable with Mr. Fitzgerald's remarks . . . that Mr. Blagojevich's conduct amounted to a 'political corruption crime spree' and 'would make Lincoln roll over in his grave,' that 'the breadth of corruption laid out in these charges is staggering,' that Mr. Blagojevich put a 'for sale' sign on the naming of a United States Senator." Those comments, Coburn wrote, "are highly inflammatory [and] clearly run afoul of the rules." The suggestion by Coburn and others that Fitzgerald's remarks had jeopardized his criminal investigation of Blagojevich is exactly what the governor's lawyers charged when they asked for Fitzgerald's removal. Still, taking on the likes of Fitzgerald was a move not many defense attorneys would choose to make. Privately, few court watchers believed there was the slightest chance this tactic would succeed. The U.S. attorney's office called the request "meritless."

Blagojevich was back in the spotlight with the convening of the Ninety-sixth General Assembly on Wednesday, January 14, 2009. As governor it was his constitutional duty to swear in the members of the Illinois Senate—the same members who were scheduled to begin his impeachment trial just twelve days later. The scene was surreal as the governor entered the magnificently restored Senate chamber. He was greeted by stone-cold silence as he made his way to the beautiful mahogany and walnut podium that overlooks the chamber. The galleries were packed, all eyes watching to see how Blagojevich would hold up under the pressure. He remained inscrutable, looking out with a steady gaze at those who were preparing the trial that could drive him from office. His voice never wavered as he asked the secretary to read the names of those who had been certified by the Board of Elections as newly elected senators.

Flowers adorned the Senate chamber; every member had brought along well-wishers. Little girls in taffeta dresses and little boys in clip-on ties crowded around their parents' Senate desks, waiting to see them take the oath of office. The atmosphere was festive, but one man could not have been enjoying the proceedings. Blagojevich adjusted his blue tie and pulled his dark suit jacket together several times, one of the few signs of the tension that crackled just below the surface. As the senators raised their hands to be sworn, few in the room could forget that their first order of business would be to act as jurors in the governor's impeachment trial.

Blagojevich quickly slipped out of the chamber after his official duties ended. Moments later the sergeants-at-arms were asked to escort the evidence in the impeachment case into the proceedings. Stacks of files were rolled in on a cart that looked like a coffin on a caisson, like a dead person being rolled up the aisle in a church funeral. "It struck me," said one state senator, "that the evidence that was rolled in like a body was the prosecutor . . . and we were the jurors."

On the same day the Senate was sworn in, the Illinois House of Representatives convened its ninety-sixth session. After House members were sworn in, the only agenda item was the reaffirmation of the impeachment vote by the preceding General Assembly. The makeup of the House had changed after the election, but the vote to impeach stayed the same—114 to 1. Newly elected representative Deborah Mell, Rod Blagojevich's sister-in-law, had wrestled with her decision on the vote. But when her sister came to her and pleaded that she vote "no," she agreed. She cast the only vote against the Article of Impeachment. Publicly she said, "The charges in the impeachment were difficult to reconcile with the man and brother-in-law I know," she said. "I could not in good conscience vote for his impeachment."

Even before the House voted on the thirteen-point Article of Impeachment, Senate leaders were quietly meeting to draw up rules for the anticipated trial. Senate president Emil Jones, one of the few politicians who continued to support the embattled governor, had not run for reelection. Jones had announced his decision to retire after the primary election, and then in time-honored Chicago fashion had installed his son Emil Jones III as the candidate for the general election. Young Jones won handily. But the new Senate president was now Chicago Democrat John Cullerton, who led the research into the rules for impeachment trials—an investigation of scanty historical evidence.

After consideration of the impeachment trial of President Bill Clinton, the Senate committee decided to pattern many of the Illinois rules after the Clinton trial since there had been little debate over the fairness of those rules. The most difficult debates, Cullerton reported, concerned the standard of proof for removal from office. Should it be "beyond a reasonable doubt," the "preponderance of the evidence," or "clear and convincing evidence"? Both in the Clinton trial and in the trail of Evan Mecham, the Arizona governor who was impeached and removed in 1988, each senator had been able to decide which of the three standards of proof he or she preferred.

The senators also decided to honor Patrick Fitzgerald's request not to subpoena witnesses who were part of Fitzgerald's criminal case. The thinking, Cullerton said, was that if an attempt were made to subpoena those witnesses, Fitzgerald would go to court to block it, resulting in months of back-and-forth legal wrangling. The government would undoubtedly win, and Blagojevich would remain in office while state government ground to a halt. Cullerton also pointed to the obvious conflict if there were an impeachment trial in progress at the same time the legislature was in session: "You say to the governor, 'Hey, Governor, are you going to sign my bill?' and he says, 'Hey, how are you going to vote on my impeachment?'"

Provisions were made to allow Blagojevich to introduce into evidence about what had been said on the public record. For instance, he could have brought in the transcript from the CBS Sunday morning show *Face the Nation*, when Rahm Emanuel said, "When I talked to Rod Blagojevich he never offered anything when we talked about the U.S. Senate seat." The rules also permitted either side to subpoena witnesses related to the five noncriminal charges in the Article of Impeachment.

Three public hearings allowed anyone, including Blagojevich's lawyers, to object to the rules. "Fundamental to our thinking—and this is what Rod Blagojevich never understood," Cullerton told me, "was that any rules we adopted, any precedents we set could potentially be used against us individually. So forget that Rod Blagojevich was clearly unpopular—we just wanted to make sure the impeachment trial was presented in a fair way."

Blagojevich's lawyers were having none of it. Calling the trial a "lynching" and comparing the tactics to those used by the federal government against supposed terrorist prisoners at Guantanamo Bay, they announced they would boycott the trial. "The rules the Senate adopted are basically unfair," lead attorney Ed Genson said. Sam Adam, Jr., called the trial "a kangaroo court. You can't possibly get any fairness out of it. It's completely un-American. We will not participate in a proceeding that completely denies the constitutional rights of the governor."

Skipping the deadline to file a witnesses list, Governor Blagojevich instead launched his defense on the airwaves.

The highly rated "Don Wade and Roma" morning talk show on conservative WLS radio was his first stop. He told his sympathetic hosts that he was dying to go to Springfield for the start of his impeachment trial, but "If I participate in that sham impeachment, which doesn't allow me to bring witnesses—a violation of the Sixth Amendment—then I will be participating in an unconstitutional activity. I will be giving credence to that unconstitutional activity, and I will undermine the people and their right to choose a governor. Now, if they make the rules fair, I'll be the first one there." The reason the legislators wanted him out, the impassioned governor told Don and Roma, "is so they could put a huge income tax increase on the people of Illinois."

Blagojevich followed his morning talk-show appearance with a full-blown press conference at the State of Illinois building. It would be the last time he would appear in the room where he had held forth for six years as governor. Passionate and populist, the governor continued to hit his main themes: He was being denied due process by not being allowed to bring in witnesses like presidential chief of staff Rahm Emanuel, or top presidential adviser Valerie Jarrett, to testify under oath that he had done nothing wrong in the process of choosing a replacement for Barack Obama's Senate seat. It was unfair to include the unproven charges from Patrick Fitzgerald's criminal complaint in the Article of Impeachment without giving him a way to challenge those charges.

In a sortie that prompted a gasp among the usually unflappable press corps, he called on the editorial board at the *Chicago Tribune* and the *Chicago Sun-Times* to help him prove his innocence and to write editorials urging the Illinois Senate to change its rules for the impeachment trial. This was the same *Tribune* editorial board whose members he had tried to get fired, according to the FBI's tape recordings in the criminal complaint.

Old cowboy movies replaced poetry as the governor sought to describe the abuse he felt had been heaped upon him by the Illinois Senate. "There was a cowboy who was charged with stealing a horse in town. And some of the other cowboys . . . were very unhappy with that guy. And one of the cowboys said, 'Let's hang him.' Then the other cowboy said, 'Hold on, before we hang him, let's give him a fair trial. Then hang him.' Under these rules, I'm not even getting a fair trial. They're just hanging me. And when they're hanging me . . . they're hanging the twelve million people of Illinois who twice have elected a governor."

The governor's media blitz exasperated the tensions among his lawyers that had been building behind the scenes. Although Genson, Adam Jr., and Sorosky had all agreed that the rules for the Senate impeachment trial were unfair, they couldn't agree on how best to deal with that. Sam Adam, Jr., advocated filing a lawsuit with the Illinois Supreme Court to try to block the start of the Senate trial. He and Sorosky also liked the idea of a media blitz where they and Blagojevich could castigate the trial as being an unfair charade is which they refused to participate. Blagojevich warmed to this idea immediately. Genson, on the other hand, strongly opposed the media blitz, feeling it would jeopardize Blagojevich's position for Fitzgerald's criminal trial.

When Blagojevich showed up on the Don and Roma show, Genson called it quits. He told Blagojevich to find a new lawyer. "I have practiced law for forty-four years. I never require a client to do what I say, but I do require clients to listen to what I say," said Genson. His departure was a significant blow for Blagojevich. The lawyers had already determined to boycott the Senate impeachment trial, but Genson was taking himself off the legal team for the expected criminal trial as well.

Part of the problem was money. Upon Blagojevich's arrest, the government had put a hold on the Friends of Blagojevich campaign fund, meaning that all expenditures had to be approved by the feds. The fund was not frozen, but it was assumed it would be when the full indictment came down. Genson had received a $500,000 advance for legal work, but the government would approve only $200,000, so Genson had to return $300,00. And there were very few options left for raising the kind of money it would take to mount a serious legal defense for the governor. Blagojevich pleaded for Genson to return, as did Adam Jr. and Sorosky, but one of the most experienced criminal defense lawyers in Chicago wished the governor well and told him, "No thanks."

Seemingly unfazed, Blagojevich pursued his media tour with obvious relish. As his appearances took on more and more of a circuslike atmosphere, he hired a press agent with experience in managing national media relations, Glenn Selig. Selig also handles the media for Drew Peterson, the suburban Chicago police sergeant whom some suspect in the murder of his third wife and the disappearance of his fourth. By this time Lucio Guerrero had taken himself out of the loop when the governor's media appearances dealt with the criminal charges. As Guerrero tried to explain to Blagojevich, he was on the state payroll as the *governor*'s press secretary, not Rod Blagojevich's press secretary, so he couldn't get involved in the proposed media blitz, though

Blagojevich pressured him to come along. "He wanted me to go to New York with him because the governor likes to be with one or two people he knows in his close groups. He didn't know Glenn Selig, who had been hired by Sam Adam Jr. who had met Selig during the R. Kelly trial."

Guerrero thought the media blitz would help Blagojevich, though he felt too many appearances were scheduled, and he says he understood the governor's reasons for wanting to plead his case in public. "I think most politicians like the spotlight, they're ego driven. His punishment will be when the spotlight is turned off and he can't get a camera. He's going to be really upset about that. When he had the opportunity to do all these things, he thought, as long as they got the name right, what does it matter? He's a charmer, and he thought he could win people over."

In his first interview with NBC's Sunday morning *Today Show*, Blagojevich was asked about his feelings the morning of his arrest. "I thought about Mandela, Dr. King, and Gandhi," he replied, "and tried to put some perspective to all this. And that is what I am doing now." He did not actually compare himself to the human rights icons, but after one news cycle most people thought he had.

As senators gathered in Springfield for the start of the governor's impeachment trial, Blagojevich continued his media rounds in New York with back-to-back appearances on ABC's *Good Morning America* and *The View*, followed by an evening date on *Larry King Live*. The telegenic governor with the good hair scored a few points as he blasted the Senate trial as a violation of his rights to due process because he could not call witnesses, could not confront the unproven criminal charges, and could not let senators hear all of the secretly recorded wiretaps.

His toughest questioning came from veteran reporter Barbara Walters on *The View*. She quizzed him hard on "selling" Barack Obama's Senate seat.

WALTERS: You've denied trying to sell President Obama's Senate seat . . . but you've been wiretapped saying, "I've got this thing—it's golden—I'm just not giving it up for nothing . . ." If that's not selling a Senate seat—what is?

BLAGOJEVICH: Well, you have to understand these were private conversations that were taking place over a long period of time. And taking snippets of conversations out of context . . .

WALTERS: Did you say it, in context, out of context—it's on a wiretap. Did you say those things? . . . Please answer . . . or why are you wasting time on these programs?

BLAGOJEVICH: Well, I think that whatever is on those tapes are—they're gonna come out, and that they'll speak for themselves. The tapes will—show the whole story.

Backstage at *The View* as at his other media stops, there was one hard and fast rule: no one touched the hair. Blagojevich was obsessive about his dark locks, which he swore had never been graced by hair dye. A black-handled hairbrush, dubbed the "football," plus at least one backup hairbrush were always available. He carried a mirror with a Velcro strap which he would attach to the nearest flat surface and continually brush his hair before any public appearance, actions he explained as merely a nervous habit.

The hair rule and his demeanor were shaken when *The View* co-host Joy Behar reached over and tousled his carefully coiffed hair on the air. Only one day into his media tour, Blagojevich was already in danger of becoming a parody of himself. *Saturday Night Live* was a given after that. For weeks a mop-haired Blagojevich look-alike opened the show, confirming that the governor of Illinois had become a national punch line.

The national media appearances continued even after the Senate trial. David Letterman asked the critical question: "Why exactly are you here, honest to God?" Trying to answer that question by dissecting Blagojevich's motives and behavior had begun well before his media tour. "Cuckoo" was Mayor Daley's analysis after Blagojevich's appearance on the Don and Roma show.

Many who had contact with Blagojevich after he became governor in fact had serious questions about his mental stability. Journalism professor and longtime Springfield observer Charles Wheeler is one of them. "I honestly think the guy is mentally ill," Wheeler said. "I think he's detached from reality. I think he's a psychopath in the sense of someone for whom the rest of the world and all other people and everything exist only to the extent that it's helpful to him. . . . He certainly is the most corrupt, least competent governor I've seen in the forty years I've been watching this stuff."

Tough analysis came from State Representative Julie Hamos as well: "I'm told his narcissism is really a critical case, that its all about him and making these points and getting on TV." Bob Arya, former senior adviser to the governor, saw Blagojevich's media blitz as one more example of his need for "adoration, adulation, and affection from people. . . . Rod liked the celebrity of being governor. Rod loved being adored by crowds. Rod loved running through parades and signing autographs and kissing babies."

According to the Mayo Clinic website, a narcissistic personality is "a mental disorder in which people have an inflated sense of their own importance and a deep need for admiration. They believe that they're superior to others and have little regard for other's people's feelings. But behind this mask of ultra-confidence lies a fragile self–esteem, vulnerable to the slightest criticism." For Arya and others, the definition fit Blagojevich to a tee. It explained his grandiosity, his dreams of being president, his eagerness to fight back when he believed he was being attacked, and his love of the limelight. In a memo to the House investigatory panel, Arya urged a psychological evaluation of Blagojevich. The panel did not follow up on his suggestion.

During his media blitz Blagojevich's legal troubles had only grown worse. Patrick Fitzgerald had agreed to release four of the FBI's wiretaps to the Illinois Senate, to be played in the impeachment trial. Fitzgerald also agreed to allow the FBI agent who had compiled the affidavit that formed the basis for the criminal complaint to testify before the Senate. The governor faced an unpleasant reckoning.

18

Final Curtain

THE CHANDELIERS that encircle the Illinois Senate gallery shimmered on the cold Monday morning of January 29, 2009, as the first trial commenced for the impeachment of an Illinois governor. Two leather desks in the Senate chamber stood empty, reserved for the governor and his attorney. The packed galleries tittered with excitement but fell into respectful silence as the solemn proceedings began.

Governor Blagojevich "repeatedly and utterly broke his oath of office, betrayed voters—and illegally used the powers of his office as a 'bargaining chip,'" intoned the House of Representatives' prosecutor David Ellis, as he began to present the evidence gathered by the House Investigative Committee to the fifty-nine senators who were acting as jurors in the trial.

One senator rose to question the Senate's use of the noncriminal evidence in the case. Rickey Hendon, an African American from Chicago's West Side, had been a consistent supporter of Blagojevich. In a later interview he told me, "In my conscience, I just could not remain totally silent on some of these issues—especially the ones that I know the Democrats in the Senate supported, like health care and flu vaccines and free rides for seniors, things like that. To me it's hypocritical to act as though we didn't support those things, or vote for those things when Emil Jones was [Senate] President." Hendon asked that the eight criminal allegations in the Article of Impeachment be separated from the remaining five charges that involved policy disputes. "To lump them all together denies Blagojevich a fair trial," Hendon told me shortly before the final vote in the Senate.

Watching from the sidelines, former Senate president Emil Jones, Jr., saw the trial as a tragic consequence of the power battle between the governor of Illinois and the speaker of the House, Mike Madigan. "All the good that [Blagojevich] has done will be forgotten. We got 'All Kids'—we got them insurance. We put more money into education than any previous administration—and all that will be forgotten, won't even be mentioned," lamented Jones. "When I look at this whole situation I understand how a lynch mob is formed. We have a lynch-mob attitude. I hate it. The legislators are looking to the next election, so they'll vote to convict. The legislators are in a hell of a box, because the frivolous charges coming out of the House will not only impact this governor, they will impact the next governor or even themselves. When they vote to impeach based on that Article of Impeachment, it will come back down on them in the future."

But when the impeachment trial began, Emil Jones, Jr., was out of power, the governor had chosen to boycott the trial, and Senator Hendon's appeal to separate the criminal charges from the noncriminal went nowhere. The governor was left without a defense. On the second day of the trial, the governor's voice finally rang out in the Senate chamber. Unfortunately it was on one on the four wiretaps released by U.S. Attorney Fitzgerald. After the tapes were played, not a single person in attendance believed that the upcoming vote to remove Governor Rod Blagojevich would not be unanimous.

Even so, the governor was not yet finished. True to form, the day before the vote to remove him from office, Blagojevich reversed his strategy and announced he would come to Springfield after all, to deliver his own closing argument. Behind the scenes his lawyers tried frantically to talk him out of it. But the governor was adamant. He wanted to tell his own story in front of the Senate and in front of the world. He would not be testifying. He would not be under oath. There would be no cross examination. But Governor Rod Blagojevich would be present, on his own terms.

As his nine-seat plane with the picture of Abraham Lincoln near its nose took off for Blagojevich's last official trip to Springfield, the governor traveled light. The notes for the speech he was about to give were tucked in one suit coat pocket, his ever-present black hairbrush in another. He was wearing one of his favorite suits, tailor made by Oxxford Clothes, a place he had patronized for years, and a silky light-blue tie. Whether he was utilizing his strong denial mechanisms or not, the governor was in amazingly good spirits as he joked with the pilots, telling them to "keep the engines running—I don't know how much longer I'm going to have the plane."

Meanwhile in the Senate chamber, the House prosecutor was preparing for his final argument. David Ellis was not nervous. After weeks of working on the case, he was familiar with the charges laid out in the Article of Impeachment in minute detail. But, like everyone in the Senate chamber that morning, he felt awed by the historic moment. In the 191 years that Illinois had been a state, a governor had never been impeached and removed from office.

Ellis took his place at the small lectern facing the jury of senators and laid out the case presented in the Article of Impeachment, that Rod Blagojevich should be removed from the Office of Governor because of a pattern of abuse of power. The chamber was silent except for the prosecutor's voice. Not one person rose to leave, and there were no whispered conversations as Ellis addressed the charges.

"The evidence shows," he intoned, "that throughout his tenure he put his own interests above the people. Which interests? The legal, personal, and political. The people of this state deserve so much better. He should be removed from office."

As Ellis's summation rang through the Senate chamber, the governor arrived in his office one floor below and began to rework the notes for his speech. He appeared calm, only his frequent calls to Patti indicating the pressure he was under. Clayton Harris, his new chief of staff, came in to tell him it was time. As the governor brushed by Harris, he confided his emotion of the moment: "Let's go home, screw it. It's not going to make a damn bit of difference anyway." Then he turned and walked toward the Senate floor.

The last words Blagojevich would speak in the Illinois Senate chamber were defiant. "There is no evidence before your body here that shows—no evidence—zero—that there was any wrongdoing by me as governor." He laid down the gauntlet to the senators, telling them what he was caught saying on tape was no different from what many of them had said in similar situations. "The evidence is four tapes. You heard those four tapes. I don't have to tell you what they say. You guys are in politics. You know what we have to do to go out and run elections. There was no criminal activity on those four tapes. You can express things in a free country, but those four tapes speak for themselves. Take those four tapes as they are and you, I believe, in fairness, will recognize and acknowledge those are conversations relating to the things all of us in politics do in order to run campaigns and try to win elections."

As an orator, Blagojevich was at the top of his game. His speech was a sad reminder of all that could have been. His notes went unread, he spoke from his heart, lashing out at the senators for denying him a fair trial. He appealed to them, saying, "Walk a mile in my shoes." He even asked for a chance to stay on as governor. He wanted "to continue to do good things for people." But there was no applause, no adulation, no standing ovation.

Although the senators were impressed by the governor's eloquence, there were unmoved by his message. And they were angered by his accusation that they all employed the same brand of politics. "People know the difference between holding a fund-raiser and asking someone to give you $100,000 or you're not going to sign their bill," Senate president John Cullerton told me. "I find that to be stunning, just stunning. I mean, I'll put it this way: no one does what he did, based on what I heard."

The governor retreated to his office where he was surrounded by staff. Guerrero recalls, "There were a lot of people crying because they realized this was the end. He thanked people—'Thanks for all the time, thanks for what you've done'—and that was it. He never said goodbye to the staff here in Chicago. I don't think he realized how many people were pulling for him, were loyal because of the things he had done and all the programs we had worked on because of him."

The attitude was far different on the Senate floor as the debate over whether to remove the governor from office began. Republican senator Matt Murphy charged that the governor "reminded us he is a really good liar. He lied about the process. He lied that the rules were unfair to him. He extorted caregivers of sick children for $50,000. He sold the U.S. Senate seat. Is there any question in anyone's mind that he must be removed from office?"

Other senators called not only for the removal of the governor but for reform of the political process in Illinois. "The problem of 'pay to play' is systemic," admitted Republican senator Susan Collins. "What is needed is meaningful campaign finance reform."

As senators continued to lambaste the governor, he slipped out the side door and headed for the airport to board the state plane. Halfway through the flight from Springfield to Chicago the phone on the plane rang—no one had ever heard that phone ring before. The governor told Guerrero not to answer it in case it was news that the vote had been taken and he was no longer governor—and no longer entitled to ride on the state plane. "I'm not jumping out," Blagojevich told Guerrero, "not for those people. I don't like heights." The phone went un-answered.

Not until several hours after Blagojevich was safely back in his Chicago home was the final vote taken. It was not a surprise.

The Illinois Senate voted 59 to 0 to remove him from office. And, in a final thrust at the man whose ambitions drove him to destroy the relationships he needed to suc-ceed, the Senate cast a second unanimous vote to bar Blagojevich from ever holding office in the State of Il-linois again.

A light, silent snow fell on Chicago that evening. Rod Blagojevich was tired. Still, he emerged from his home to make one more proclamation to those assembled. His security detail had been pulled, and Guerrero was no longer available to rein in the press. The result was chaos, with reporters and camera crews pushing and shoving while Blagojevich plunged into the crowd toward a group of neighborhood children. A boy shouted out to him, "You're the greatest. Will you have time to play ball with me now?"

"Sure, I will," said Blagojevich. But he put others on notice: "Just because I'm not the governor anymore, doesn't mean I'm going to stop fighting." As his words faded into the cold Chicago night, the son of immigrants, who had risen to become governor of Illinois, retreated into his dark and silent home.

Epilogue

THE SAGA of Roland Burris and the U.S. Senate seat did not end with his swearing in. New questions were raised about whether "pay to play" was involved when Governor Blagojevich tapped Burris for Barack Obama's vacant seat. In testimony before the Illinois House Investigative Committee on January 8, 2009, Burris had assured the members that he had spoken only with former Blagojevich chief of staff and lobbyist Lon Monk about his interest in being appointed senator. But in a follow-up affidavit requested by the committee, Burris revealed that he had had conversations with Blagojevich's brother Robert in October and November about raising money for the governor. Burris initially had told Robert Blagojevich he would like to help the governor raise campaign funds, then said he was unable to pull in any money because of the governor's unpopularity.

Because Burris was under oath before the House impeachment panel, the state's attorney of Sangamon County, where Springfield is located, opened a perjury investigation into Burris's conflicting statements. The U.S. Senate Ethics Committee also began a probe of Senator Burris's conduct. Calls for Burris to step down as senator came from Illinois' senior senator Dick Durbin, new Illinois governor Pat Quinn, and many others. But Senator Burris remained firm. It is unlikely that he will be dislodged from his Senate seat, though his chances for election in 2010 appear severely damaged.

As this book went to press, U.S. Attorney Patrick Fitzgerald had not yet obtained a criminal indictment against Rod Blagojevich from a grand jury. There is little doubt, however, that an extensive criminal indictment will be returned, elaborating and perhaps adding to the charges raised in the criminal complaint that led to the governor's arrest.

Index

Index

Daley, Richard M., 19, 49, 51–52, 70, 115, 226; contributions, ban on, 28; and political patronage, 24, 27; Shakman Decrees, challenging of, 24

Davis, Danny, 168, 197, 201

Degnan, Tim, 130

Democratic Congressional Campaign Committee, 87

Democratic National Convention, 62, 63

Demuzio, Vince, 125

Department of Homeland Security, 212

Despres, Leon, 17–18

Dirksen, Everett McKinley, 6

Dold, Bruce, 183

Draskovic, Vuk, 75–76

Durbin, Dick, 190, 192–193, 201, 203, 236

Dylan, Bob, 40

Ecosse Hospital Products, 141–142

Edgar, Jim, 157

Edward Hospital, 99, 101

Eisendrath, Edwin, 156

Eisenhower, Dwight D., 37

Eleventh Ward, 25–26, 116

Ellis, David, 205, 228, 231

Emanuel, Rahm, 143–144, 175–176, 209–210, 220–221

England: and flu vaccine, 140, 210

Everett, Marge Lindheimer, 22

Family Care Health Insurance, 151, 210, 213

First Ward, 13; and First Ward Ball, 14

Fitzgerald, Patrick, 24, 35, 41, 48, 85, 88, 106, 120, 134, 190–191, 227, 230, 236; as apolitical, 10; background of, 8–9; criticism of, 216–217; federal complaint of, 206–207, 221; as modern-day Eliot Ness, 7; as overzealous, 11, 26; political corruption, investigations of, 7, 8, 12, 90–91, 96, 98, 113–114, 154–155, 161, 167, 169, 170–171, 180, 187; and political patronage, 25–27; and George Ryan, 28–31; and Shakman Decrees, 25; as special counsel, 11; and Edward Vrdolyak, 50–51; witnesses, subpoenaing of, 209–210, 219. See also Operation Board Games

Fitzgerald, Peter, 7, 8

Flanagan, Michael, 69–71

Flu vaccine, 140–141

Food and Drug Administration (FDA): and flu vaccine shortage, 140–142; and low-cost prescription drugs, 143–144

Foster, John H., 106

Franks, Jack, 212

Friends of Blagojevich, 168–170, 223

Index

A NOTE ON THE AUTHOR

Elizabeth Brackett is a correspondent for PBS's *The NewsHour with Jim Lehrer*, reporting on national politics, finance, the environment, science, and sports. She has won a Peabody Award for her political reporting as well as a National Emmy. Ms. Brackett also is a news host for *Chicago Tonight*, the flagship public affairs program on WTTW, the PBS affiliate in Illinois. A lifetime Chicagoan, she has been a social worker and community organizer, and worked in mayoral and presidential campaigns before becoming a broadcast journalist. Ms. Brackett is also U.S.A. Triathlon age group national champion and a member of the U.S. national team. She lives with her husband in the Hyde Park neighborhood of Chicago.